At Issue

I Cancer

Other Books in the At Issue Series:

Are Athletes Good Role Models?

Are Natural Disasters Increasing?

The Energy Crisis

How Safe Is America's Infrastructure?

Hurricane Katrina

Is Childhood Becoming Too Sexualized?

Piracy on the High Seas

Polygamy

Should the Internet Be Free?

Should the U.S. Close Its Borders?

Should Vaccinations Be Mandatory?

Teen Smoking

What Is the Impact of E-Waste?

What Is the Impact of Tourism?

What Role Should the U.S. Play in the Middle East?

At Issue

| Cancer

Jacqueline Langwith, Book Editor

GREENHAVEN PRESS
A part of Gale, Cengage Learning

 GALE
CENGAGE Learning·

Detroit • New York • San Francisco • New Haven, Conn • Waterville, Maine • London

Elizabeth Des Chenes, *Managing Editor*

© 2012 Greenhaven Press, a part of Gale, Cengage Learning.

Gale and Greenhaven Press are registered trademarks used herein under license.

For more information, contact:
Greenhaven Press
27500 Drake Rd.
Farmington Hills, MI 48331-3535
Or you can visit our Internet site at gale.cengage.com

For product information and technology assistance, contact us at

Gale Customer Support, 1-800-877-4253
For permission to use material from this text or product, submit all requests online at
www.cengage.com/permissions

Further permissions questions can be e-mailed to permissionrequest@cengage.com

Articles in Greenhaven Press anthologies are often edited for length to meet page requirements. In addition, original titles of these works are changed to clearly present the main thesis and to explicitly indicate the author's opinion. Every effort is made to ensure that Greenhaven Press accurately reflects the original intent of the authors. Every effort has been made to trace the owners of copyrighted material.

Cover image © Images.com/Corbis.

LIBRARY OF CONGRESS CATALOGING-IN-PUBLICATION DATA

Cancer / Jacqueline Langwith, book editor.
      p. cm. -- (At issue)
   Includes bibliographical references and index.
   ISBN 978-0-7377-5558-9 (hardcover) -- ISBN 978-0-7377-5559-6 (pbk.)
   1. Cancer--Prevention. 2. Carcinogens. 3. Cancer vaccines. I. Langwith, Jacqueline.
   RC268.C332 2012
   616.99'405--dc23

                                                                    2012001664

Printed in the United States of America
   2 3 4 5 6   16 15 14 13 12

FD184

Contents

Introduction   7

1. Genes Cause Cancer   10
   American Society of Clinical Oncology

2. The Modern Environment   14
   Causes Cancer
   Heidi Stevenson

3. Vitamin D Reduces the Risk   18
   of Cancer
   Vitamin D Council

4. The Role of Vitamin D in Cancer   23
   Prevention Is Unclear
   Joanne Nicholas

5. Mammograms Can Save Lives   28
   Daniel B. Kopans

6. Mammograms Do Not Save Lives   32
   Veneta Masson

7. Lifestyle and Spirituality Are Important   41
   for Treating Cancer
   Deborah A. Ray

8. Artificial Intelligence Can Help Find   48
   a Cure for Cancer
   Jay M. Tenenbaum and Jeff Shrager

9. Cancer Will Likely Become a Chronic,   58
   Manageable Disease
   David Godkin

10. Lung Cancer Research Is Underfunded 69
   Onkar Khullar and Yolonda L. Colson

11. Cancer Research Receives More Funding 73
   than Heart Research
   Shelley Wood

Organizations to Contact 80

Bibliography 86

Index 91

Introduction

A vaccine to help prevent cancer was a hot button issue during the campaign to choose the Republican nominee for the 2012 US Presidential election. The issue focused on Texas Governor Rick Perry's executive order to mandate inoculation of preadolescent girls against a sexually transmitted disease—human papillomavirus (HPV)—that is strongly linked to cervical cancer. Perry's order was never implemented. However, Michele Bachmann, a US congresswoman from Minnesota and one-time candidate for the Republican presidential nomination, suggested that the HPV vaccine was unsafe and Perry was wrongly trying to force it on young girls. Bachmann's comments were roundly condemned by the medical community. Although no vaccination is risk-free, experts insist, the HPV vaccine is generally considered safe. The vaccine is recommended by the American Academy of Pediatrics and the American Cancer Society as an effective prevention of cervical cancer.[1] Because of the attention paid in the media to Bachmann's assertions, the HPV vaccine may be the most well-known cancer vaccine. However it is just one of several vaccines that scientists are developing to fight cancer.

Most cancer vaccines target cancer-causing pathogens, or microbes, such as viruses or bacteria. Several cancers are linked to microbes. For instance, cervical cancer, as well as vaginal cancer, penile cancer, and cancers of the upper throat are linked to HPV. Liver cancer is associated with the hepatitis B and C viruses. Hodgkin's lymphoma is connected with the Epstein-Barr virus and stomach cancer is associated with *Helicobacter pylori* viral infections. Other cancers associated with microbes include bladder cancer, Kaposi's sarcoma, and adult T-cell leukemia.

1. William Schaffner, "Repeat After Me: HPV Vaccine is an Anti-Cancer Vaccine," *Huffington Post*, November 14, 2011. www.huffingtonpost.com.

Vaccines against cancer-causing microbes are like conventional vaccines, such as the seasonal flu vaccine, or the familiar vaccines that children get for childhood diseases. Generally, these vaccines are composed of an inactivated or killed pathogen, or a particle from the pathogen. The goal of these vaccines is to stimulate the immune system to manufacture antibodies that will recognize the pathogen in future exposures and mount a successful immune response against it. These vaccines prevent cancer by protecting people from being infected with a cancer-causing microbe.

Other types of cancer vaccines are being developed to treat, rather than prevent, cancer. These vaccines are known as therapeutic cancer vaccines. Scientists have long known that the immune system recognizes and tries to destroy cancer cells. However, generally the immune response is too weak to fight the tumor-producing cells and cancer develops. The administration of a vaccine to strengthen the immune response in people already battling cancer is a type of treatment known as immunotherapy.

Therapeutic cancer vaccines work to train a cancer patient's immune system to mount a strong immune response against the cancerous cells invading his or her body. It is hoped that the patient's newly educated immune system will beat back the cancer by destroying cancerous cells as soon as they are produced, or weaken the cancer so that it will be more susceptible to chemotherapy or radiation treatment. It is also hoped that the antibodies created by the immune system will be able to recognize and destroy the cancer cells for years to come and help keep cancer from coming back.

The first therapeutic vaccine approved for use in the US was Provenge. The US Food and Drug Administration (FDA) approved Provenge for the treatment of advanced prostate cancer in April 2010. Provenge is not like other medications that are made in bulk. Provenge is tailor-made for each patient. A small sample of immune cells is collected from the patient and then exposed to prostate cancer cells in the laboratory. The stimulated immune cells, or antibodies, are then injected back into the patient. It is hoped that the antibodies will kick-start the patient's own immune system to mount an effective attack on the cancer. William Haseltine is one of the pioneering scientists behind the therapeutic cancer vaccine concept and cofounded the company that developed Provenge. Upon the FDA's approval of Provenge, Haseltine wrote about the vaccine's role in the war against cancer. Writing in the journal the *Atlantic*, Haseltine said, "This small step in cancer treatment for men with advanced prostate cancer provides new hope for all those with cancer. We have begun to realize the dream of harnessing the power of the immune system to fight cancer. The road to here has been long and circuitous, but the path ahead is clear."[2]

Cancer vaccines are just one of the many research avenues scientists are exploring in the quest to eradicate a disease that has inflicted an enormous toll on humanity. In *At Issue: Cancer* doctors, scientists, and others discuss and debate other cancer treatment approaches, what causes cancer, whether or not cancer will ever be cured, and other issues surrounding this deadly disease.

---

2. William Haseltine, "America's First Therapeutic Cancer Vaccine," *The Atlantic*, May 1, 2010.

1

Genes Cause Cancer

American Society of Clinical Oncology

The American Society of Clinical Oncology (ASCO) is a non-profit organization dedicated to improving cancer care and prevention. ASCO members include physicians and health care professionals in all levels of the field of oncology.

Modern medicine has discovered that cancer is a genetic disease. Genes are the building blocks of life, providing instructions that keep the entire body functioning. However, genes can acquire mistakes, or mutations, and these mutations can lead to various cancers. Tumor suppressor genes, oncogenes, and DNA repair genes can all play a role in causing cancer.

The ancient Greeks believed that cancer was caused by too much body fluid they called "black bile." Doctors in the seventeenth and eighteenth centuries suggested that parasites caused cancer. Today, doctors understand that cancer is genetic, meaning that changes to various genes in the body can lead to cancer.

Genes and Chromosomes

Genes are the basic functional and physical units of heredity that are passed from parent to child. They are made of deoxyribonucleic acid (DNA) and are located on structures called chromosomes located in every cell of a person's body. Genes provide the instructions to keep your body functioning. Most

American Society of Clinical Oncology, "The Genetics of Cancer," August 13, 2009. www .cancer.net. © 2009 American Society of Clinical Oncology. All rights reserved. Reprinted with permission.

people are familiar with genes for their role in determining a person's physical characteristics, such as eye color.

The human body contains nearly 30,000 genes. They are located on 46 chromosomes and arranged in 23 pairs. Chromosome pairs are numbered 1 through 22 and are called autosomes. The remaining two chromosomes (the 23rd pair) are the sex chromosomes, which determine whether someone is born female or male. Because genes come in pairs, a person inherits one gene in each pair from the mother and the other from the father.

Usually it takes multiple mutations over a lifetime to produce a cancer cell. This is why cancer occurs more often in older people—there have been more opportunities for mutations to accumulate.

The Role of Genes in Cancer

In a person's body, cells are continually dying and being replaced. For example, cells in the skin, liver, and intestines are replaced every few weeks. The body makes new cells by copying the old cells, and in this process (called cell division), there may be mistakes in how the genetic material is copied. These are called mutations. Some mutations have no effect on a cell, while other mutations are harmful or helpful to the cell. If a mutation is not corrected, and it occurs in a critical part of the gene, it may lead to cancer. However, the chance of one mutation leading to cancer is rare. Usually it takes multiple mutations over a lifetime to produce a cancer cell. This is why cancer occurs more often in older people—there have been more opportunities for mutations to accumulate.

There are two basic kinds of genetic mutations. If the mutation is directly passed from a parent to a child, it is called a germline mutation. This means that the mutation is present in every cell of the child's body, including the reproductive sperm and egg cells. Because the mutation affects reproductive cells, it is passed from generation to generation. Germline mutations are responsible for 5% to 10% of cancer cases, which is called familial (occurring in families) cancer.

Acquired mutations occur during a person's life and are not passed from parent to child. These mutations are caused by tobacco, UV radiation, viruses, age, and other factors. Cancer caused by this type of mutation is called sporadic cancer, which is much more common than familial cancer.

Most scientists believe that cancer happens when several genes of a particular group of cells become mutated. Some people may have more inherited mutations than others, and even with the same amount of environmental exposure, some people are simply more likely to develop cancer.

Genes That Play a Role in Cancer

The following types of genes contribute to cancer:

- Tumor suppressor genes are protective genes. Normally, they suppress (limit) cell growth by monitoring the rate at which cells divide into new cells, repairing mismatched DNA (a cause of mutations), and controlling cell death. When a tumor suppressor gene is mutated (due to heredity or environmental factors), cells continue to grow and can eventually form a tumor. *BRCA1, BRCA2,* and *p53* are examples of tumor suppressor genes. In fact, nearly 50% of all cancers involve a missing or damaged *p53* gene.

- Oncogenes turn a healthy cell into a cancerous one. *HER2/neu* and *ras* are two common oncogenes.

- DNA repair genes fix any mistakes made when DNA is replicated (copied). Mistakes that aren't fixed become mutations, which may eventually lead to cancer, especially if the mutation occurs in a tumor suppressor gene or oncogene.

Cancer develops when several genes in a cell become mutated in a way that overrides the checks and balances of the cell. However, many cancers cannot be tied to a specific gene, and some genes may interact in unpredictable ways with other genes or factors in the environment to cause cancer. In the future, doctors hope to learn more about the role of genetic changes in the development of cancer, which may lead to improved cancer treatment and prevention strategies.

2

The Modern Environment Causes Cancer

Heidi Stevenson

Heidi Stevenson is a homeopathic practitioner in Scotland. She also operates the website Gaia-health.com, where she writes articles on subjects ranging from health to issues about living in the modern world.

Scientists have found strong evidence indicating that cancer is a disease of the modern world. The scientists studied ancient Egyptian mummies and found them absent of any tumors, even though tumors should be preserved in the mummification process. It is nonsense to attribute the lack of tumors in Ancient Egyptians to short life spans, as some people do. It is clear that cancer is caused not by genes, but by our modern industrial world.

Forget all that nonsense about the search for the cure for cancer. It will never be found. The search for a cure is nothing but redirection from the reality that cancer is caused by modern life. It isn't in your genes. It isn't ever going to be cured. It's an internal effect of the world we've created—and symbolic of our destruction of the natural world.

A study, entitled "Cancer: an old disease, a new disease or something in between?" was done by A. Rosalie David and Michael R. Zimmerman of the University of Manchester KNH Centre for Biomedical Egyptology. Published in the journal

Nature Reviews Cancer, it strongly suggests that cancer is a disease of the modern world. It is, of course, controversial.

No Cancer in Ancient Societies

The study investigated Egyptian mummies. The authors noted that the written records show little evidence for cancer. They also noted that tests demonstrate that tumors are preserved through the mummification process. Zimmerman stated:

> In an ancient society lacking surgical intervention, evidence of cancer should remain in all cases. The virtual absence of malignancies in mummies must be interpreted as indicating their rarity in antiquity, indicating that cancer causing factors are limited to societies affected by modern industrialization.

Of course, the deniers are out in force. The usual nonsensical claim—never proven—is that a lack of cancer in premodern times is the result of short lifespans. However, that simply isn't true. As [this author] noted in *Heart Attack Is a Disease of Agribusiness, Not Longevity*, [on August 16, 2010] modern societies that are not exposed to modern chemicals and agribusiness food almost never suffer from either heart disease or cancer, no matter how long they live.

There is no evidence to suggest that cancer and most other chronic diseases are anything but a modern plague, created by the modern world.

Another point that is generally missed by those who claim that people didn't get cancer because they didn't live long enough is the skewing of statistics. While it's true that the average lifespan was shorter, those who survived childhood tended to live far longer than most of us today realize, often achieving the same lifespans we enjoy today. Yet, they rarely succumbed to cancer.

David and Zimmerman decided to look at mummified remains because of the claim that the only reason there is little evidence of cancer in ancient people is that tumors must not survive over time—though they have no explanation for why that would be, when nontumorous tissues do survive.

Professor David stated:

The ancient Egyptian data offers both physical and literary evidence, giving a unique opportunity to look at the diseases they had and the treatments they tried. They were the fathers of pharmacology so some treatments did work.

They were very inventive and some treatments thought of as magical were genuine therapeutic remedies. For example, celery was used to treat rheumatism back then and is being investigated today....

Their surgery and the binding of fractures were excellent because they knew their anatomy: there was no taboo on working with human bodies because of mummification. They were very hands-on and it gave them a different mindset to working with bodies than the Greeks, who had to come to Alexandria to study medicine.

Yet again extensive ancient Egyptian data, along with other data from across the millennia, has given modern society a clear message—cancer is man-made and something that we can and should address.

As previously discussed by Gaia Health, there is no evidence to suggest that cancer and most other chronic diseases are anything but a modern plague, created by the modern world.

It Is Time to Focus on Cancer's True Causes

Isn't it well past time that we focused attention on the genuine causes of cancer? The massive amount of money and effort that's going into studying genetics, trying to place the blame for individual cases on so-called flawed genes, is a complete waste. It cannot provide serious benefit, because the evidence exists that cancer is not a genetic disease. It's a disease of modern times.

It's well past time that our health agencies insist on proof that products do not cause cancer—among other diseases. Instead, they're allowed to proliferate while others attempt to prove what we already know: modern chemicals, plastics, pesticides, fertilizers, drugs, lack of sunlight (vitamin D) and stress are causing cancer and other life-destroying diseases.

3

Vitamin D Reduces the Risk of Cancer

Vitamin D Council

The Vitamin D Council is a nonprofit, educational corporation in the State of California, founded in 2003 by John Cannell. The stated mission of the Council is to end the worldwide vitamin D deficiency epidemic by means of outreach and awareness, treatment, research, and activism.

Cancer is a leading cause of death worldwide. It is associated with several risk factors, such as environmental toxins, smoking, obesity, and diet. Evidence shows that Vitamin D can reduce the risk of many types of cancer. However, the vitamin provides the strongest benefit for people at risk for colon, rectal, and breast cancer.

Cancer is the uncontrolled growth of abnormal cells that can occur anywhere in the body when damaged cells fail to undergo apoptosis, or programmed cell death. Oftentimes, cancer begins in one area of the body and then spreads to one or more other areas, a process known as metastasis.

A leading cause of death world-wide, the number of deaths due to cancer are expected to increase to an estimated 12 million by the year 2030.

Risk Factors

The most commonly-recognized risk factors for cancer are:

- Environmental toxins

- Smoking

- Alcohol consumption

- Obesity

- Lack of exercise

But there are other known, less-recognized, risk factors.

High intake of meat and dairy

Eating a diet high in animal products early in life causes the body to produce more insulin-like growth factor (IGF). IGF helps the body grow, but it also helps tumors grow. Many cancers that are prevalent in the United States and Europe are uncommon in developing countries that do not have high amounts of animal products in their diet. Such countries who have Westernized their diets have had dramatic increases in their cancer rates.

Sunlight exposure and cancer risk

Sunlight has a direct effect on reducing risk of many types of cancer. The shortwave ultraviolet portion of sunlight, ultraviolet-B (UVB), stimulates the body to produce vitamin D, which protects against cancer.

Solar ultraviolet light is also a risk factor for skin cancer and melanoma. The risk of skin cancer is highest for people with pale skin, who have sunburned a number of times, or who spend a lot of time in the sun for work or other reasons. Those who work in the sun generally do not have an increased risk of melanoma.

The number of cancer cases and deaths vary with the amount of regional sunlight for many types of cancer. According to cancer studies, there are:

- Lower rates in the sunny Southwest United States and higher rates in the darker Northeast

- Higher rates in countries that are farther from the equator and receive less sunlight

Vitamin D and Cancer

Vitamin D reduces the risk of many types of cancer. The evidence comes from the following numerous types of studies:

- Ecological studies, [which] define populations geographically such as by state or country, generally find lower cancer incidence or mortality rates in regions that have more solar UVB or are closer to the equator.

- Observational studies compare people with cancer to those without the disease. Studies that use short intervals between vitamin D intake or blood levels and cancer incidence are more likely to find the effect of vitamin D on cancer risk since vitamin D levels MAY change with time.

- One randomized controlled trial of vitamin D supplementation confirmed the benefits in reducing risk of cancer for those taking vitamin D compared to those not taking vitamin D.

- In addition, numerous laboratory studies have been done to investigate the mechanisms of vitamin D in reducing risk of cancer incidence, growth, and spread.

The evidence of vitamin D benefits is strongest for colon, rectal, and breast cancer. Vitamin D also protects against cancer of the bladder, brain, endometrial lining, esophagus, gallbladder, kidney, lungs, ovaries, pancreas, prostate, and stomach. In addition, vitamin D protects against Hodgkin's and non-Hodgkin's lymphoma, leukemia, multiple myeloma, and melanoma.

Vitamin D levels greater than 40 ng/mL [nanograms per milliliter] reduce the risk of cancer.

The rates of breast, colon, and rectal cancer decrease rapidly as vitamin D levels increase from very low levels [less than 10 ng/ml] out to 20–30 ng/ml, then decreases at a slower rate until levels reach about 50 ng/ml. No comparable findings have been reported for other types of cancer. However, it is assumed that they behave in a similar manner since incidence and mortality rates are similar in geographical studies.

High levels of vitamin D are associated with a lower risk of many types of cancer in both observational studies on individuals and geographic studies of populations.

Vitamin D has been shown to block the growth of cancer tumors. Calcitriol, an active form of vitamin D, is produced by the body by various organs after vitamin D is processed by the liver. Calcitriol provides numerous benefits against cancer. This form of vitamin D encourages cells to either adapt to their organ or commit apoptosis [cell death]. Calcitriol also limits blood supply to the tumor and reduces the spread of cancer.

High levels of vitamin D are associated with a lower risk of many types of cancer in both observational studies on individuals and geographic studies of populations.

Based on studies of breast, colon, and rectal cancer, vitamin D levels of 40–60 ng/mL reduce the risk of cancer. Taking 1000–4000 international units (IU) (25–100 mcg micrograms)/day of vitamin D is associated with reduced breast cancer risk.

Studies have shown that taking both vitamin D and calcium provides additional cancer protection for many types of cancer. Calcium intake of more than 1000 mg [milligrams]/day from either diet or supplements is recommended.

Patients in one study took daily doses of 1100 IU (27.5 mcg) vitamin D and 1450 mg calcium. These patients had a

77% reduction in the incidence of all types of cancer between the ends of the first and fourth years of the study compared to those taking a placebo.

People with higher vitamin D levels at time of cancer diagnosis often have a higher survival rate. This has been verified for people with breast, colorectal, lung, and prostate cancer; non-Hodgkin's lymphoma; and melanoma. These studies suggest that increasing vitamin D levels after cancer diagnosis may improve chances of survival.

Some cancer treatment centers are now giving at least 5000 IU (125 mcg)/day vitamin D to patients with cancer. Outcome results have yet to be published.

4

The Role of Vitamin D in Cancer Prevention Is Unclear

Joanne Nicholas

Joanne Nicholas is a press officer for three hospitals in New York. She is also a health and medical writer, specializing in cancer and cancer policy issues. The Journal of the National Cancer Institute *was created in the 1940s to focus attention specifically on cancer-related scientific papers.*

Vitamin D is an important part of the diet and federal scientists are recommending that Americans increase their intake of this vitamin. However, federal scientists have also concluded that there just isn't enough evidence to show that Vitamin D can reduce the risk of cancer. Scientists are hopeful that the VITAL Trial, a large-scale trial testing Vitamin D's role in the prevention of cancer, heart disease, and stroke, can provide conclusive results. Other studies are also being undertaken that are looking at Vitamin D's role in preventing specific cancers, such as prostate and breast cancers. Still, some researchers question whether any of these studies are accurately measuring Vitamin D's cancer prevention impacts.

About one-third of Americans are not getting enough vitamin D, according to a March [2011] report from the Centers for Disease Control and Prevention. That conclusion came about 6 months after the Institute of Medicine (IOM) issued new recommendations increasing the dietary reference intakes for vitamin D.

Notably absent from both reports were recommendations regarding vitamin D's relationship to cancer.

For years, some studies have suggested that vitamin D intake is associated with reduced risk of cancer—articularly colorectal cancer but also breast, prostate, and pancreatic cancers. The findings have attracted media attention and raised hope that vitamin D supplements could ward off the disease. But other studies, including some large ones, have had conflicting results.

As a result, the IOM concluded that the evidence to date is too weak to make recommendations regarding vitamin D and cancer. "The role of vitamin D in both prevention and treatment of cancer remains a work in progress," said IOM committee member JoAnn E. Manson, M.D., Dr. P.H., who cowrote a commentary on vitamin D and cancer in the *New England Journal of Medicine* in March, "We have seen this excitement before with beta-carotene, vitamin E, folate, and selenium," said Manson, a professor at Harvard Medical School. "It is important that the enthusiasm not outpace the evidence as shown."

The evidence to date is too weak to make recommendations regarding vitamin D and cancer.

Nevertheless, research on vitamin D and disease goes on. A look at the National Institutes of Health Clinical Trials website during the first week of May showed 1,326 trials assessing vitamin D's effects on cancer, pregnant women, the elderly, African Americans, patients with HIV, prediabetes, heart disease, lupus, rheumatoid arthritis, cystic fibrosis, the obese, the mentally ill, and more.

The VITAL Trial

Amid the many studies under way is a newly launched, large multicenter trial called VITAL (Vitamin D and Omega-3 Trial), investigating whether high doses of vitamin D and the omega-3 fatty acids found in fish oil can reduce the risk of developing cancer, heart disease, and stroke. Primary outcomes are incidence of these diseases after 5 years.

VITAL is the first large-scale randomized trial designed to test vitamin D's role in preventing cancer and cardiovascular disease, Manson said. The trial is testing a higher dose of vitamin D than most previous studies and is "large enough to provide conclusive results."

In mid-2010, the trial began recruiting 20,000 U.S. men aged 60 years and over and women aged 65 and older, and enrollment will continue through 2011. The basically healthy participants, with no history of cancer or cardiovascular disease, will receive two pills per day in one of the following combinations: vitamin D_3 and fish oil, vitamin D_3 and fish oil placebo, vitamin D_3 placebo and fish oil, or both placebos. (Vitamin D_3 dose is 2,000 IU; fish oil dose is 1 g [gram].) They will be monitored for 5 years and will be asked to complete an annual questionnaire about health, lifestyle habits, smoking, medication, and new medical diagnoses. Consent for medical record review will be requested to confirm health outcomes.

In addition to VITAL, several smaller trials are looking at specific questions related to vitamin D and cancer. Some are focusing on the vitamin in cancer patients. For example, at Memorial Sloan-Kettering Cancer Center in New York, researchers are investigating the effects, good or bad, that vitamin D levels have on stage IV colorectal cancer; a multicenter trial led by the University of Toronto and Mount Sinai Hospital in New York is investigating vitamin D's effects on prostate cancer-associated lesions and on vitamin D metabolites in prostate tissue; and a study by Stanford University and the Department of Defense is assessing whether vitamin D levels affect the characteristics of a woman's breast cancer at diagnosis and whether a short course of vitamin D in women with low levels changes the gene expression of their breast cancers.

Other key questions must also be addressed, said Steven K. Clinton, M.D., Ph.D., a professor in the division of medical oncology at Ohio State University in Columbus and a member of the IOM Committee. "For example, we need studies of how vitamin D impacts the efficacy of cancer therapy and its toxicity. In addition, many past studies do not differentiate between vitamin D alone and vitamin D plus calcium, so we need to examine the optimal intake of each nutrient independently."

Design Flaw?

But additional studies may be definitive only if they are measuring vitamin D intake in the right populations. A commentary published in the *Journal of the American Medical Association* in April by Martha Clare Morris, Sc.D., and Christine C. Tangney, Ph.D., of Rush University Medical Center in Chicago, suggests that a design flaw in randomized trials of vitamin supplements may be responsible for many studies' negative findings.

"Vitamin treatment may not be effective in these trials because nutrient intake among the participants is already at optimal levels," Morris wrote in an e-mail. "Public health may be better served by initially conducting trials in individuals with insufficient levels of the vitamin studied and, if effective, to then test people with adequate levels."

Morris said she is unaware of trials of vitamin D and cancer risk reduction that are restricting eligibility to people with low levels of the vitamin. But she believes that could be an important criterion for patient selection.

"I am in discussion with various experts across multiple fields on this topic," Morris said, and she hopes to convene a conference "whose goal would be to come up with more appropriate approaches for examining nutritional relations with disease in both randomized trials and epidemiological studies and to make recommendations for how to establish best evidence in nutritional science."

5

Mammograms Can Save Lives

Daniel B. Kopans

Daniel B. Kopans is a professor in the Department of Radiology at Harvard Medical School and the Director and founder of the Breast Imaging Division in the Department of Radiology at Massachusetts General Hospital. He is the author the textbook Breast Imaging *and has authored over 200 scientific articles.*

The 2009 US Preventive Services Task Force (USPSTF) guidelines, which call for a decrease in routine breast cancer screening, are based on flawed evidence and should be rescinded. The USPSTF says women between the ages of 40 and 49 should not be offered routine mammograms and women 50 and older should only be screened every two years. These recommendations take away a woman's choice to decide for herself whether she wants to be screened, they place women at risk of developing incurable cancer, and they contradict studies which clearly show that mammograms save lives.

In November 2009, the US Preventive Services Task Force (USPSTF) withdrew its support for mammographic screening for women aged 40 to 49 years and recommended that women aged 50 to 74 years be screened every 2 years. It is unclear why the USPSTF decided to drop its support, considering that the only important new data that have become available since 1997 (when the National Cancer Institute once again supported screening beginning at the age of 40 years)

Daniel B. Kopans, "The Recent US Preventive Services Task Force Guidelines Are Not Supported by the Scientific Evidence and Should Be Rescinded," *Journal of the American College of Radiology*, April 2010. All rights reserved. Reproduced with permission.

are national statistics showing that as more women participate in mammographic screening, the death rate from breast cancer continues to decrease. The USPSTF, incongruously, agreed that screening is saving lives but decided that it would make the decision for women in their 40s because the members felt that the "harms" of screening (anxiety from having the test, breast compression, false-positive results, needle biopsies, and possible overtreatment) were worse than allowing women to die from breast cancer. These guidelines will likely result in women being advised by their doctors, who rely on the advice of the USPSTF, to forgo mammography screening. Perhaps an even greater risk is that insurance companies, citing these guidelines, may no longer pay for screening before age 50 and only every 2 years from 50 to 74, essentially denying access to screening for many women. The medical community has made cogent arguments in support of providing patients with information so that they can make "informed decisions," but the USPSTF has taken the decision to participate in mammographic screening away from women.

The USPSTF even acknowledges in its discussion that screening every 2 years, instead of annually, will result in unnecessary deaths that could be avoided with annual screening.

Unfortunate Consequences

It is clear that the USPSTF did not think through the consequences of its guidelines. In addition to denying women in their 40s access to mammographic screening, the agency also told women in their 40s that they should not perform breast self-examinations and should not allow trained health care professionals to perform clinical breast examinations. What does this leave for women in their 40s? The USPSTF is telling women to wait until their cancers are so large that they can no longer ignore them and then bring them to their doctors' attention, when there is no longer a chance for cure. Is this what we should advise our patients?

Furthermore, the USPSTF is withdrawing support for screening women aged 50 to 74 years annually, advising instead that they can wait 2 years between mammograms, essentially saying that it is fine to allow their cancers to grow for an additional year before they are diagnosed. The USPSTF even acknowledges in its discussion that screening every 2 years, instead of annually, will result in unnecessary deaths that could be avoided with annual screening, but the agency found this to be reasonable because it reduces the false-positive rate.

The USPSTF has misled American women and their physicians by suggesting that they have reviewed all of the pertinent literature and data on breast cancer screening and that their guidelines are "evidence based." In fact, the USPSTF has selected the information that suits its agenda. The death rate from breast cancer has decreased by 30% since 1990. This is directly linked to the onset of annual mammographic screening for women aged $\geq$ 40 years in the mid-1980s. Before mammographic screening, nothing had influenced the death rate since 1940.

The marked decrease in deaths that accompanies mammographic screening has been a major advance for women's health.

Evidence Supports Screening

Studies in Sweden and the Netherlands have clearly shown that when mammographic screening is introduced into the general population, the vast majority of the subsequent decrease in deaths is due to mammographic screening, not to new therapies. Completely ignoring these direct measures, the USPSTF has chosen to rely on its own computer models, not even mentioning that other computer models disagree with its conclusions. What the agency has done is comparable to stating that because sophisticated financial computer models predicted that the economy was sound in the fall of 2008, the financial collapse must not have happened. There is no justification for relying on computer models when there are direct data that bear on the question.

By relying on the number of screening studies needed to save one life, the USPSTF is clearly sending the message that it does not think that it is worth saving women in their 40s, but the agency does not have the honesty to state this directly. If cost is the issue, then the USPSTF needs to factor in the cost of allowing breast cancers to be advanced before they are treated (necessitating more morbid and expensive therapy), not to mention the costs to their families and society of losing these women. The agency needs to allow women to decide what is a reasonable cost and not deny them access to screening simply because it does not feel that it is worth saving women from dying of breast cancer. True cost-benefit analysis was performed in 1994, when the National Cancer Institute promulgated the exact same guidelines. At that time, screening beginning at the age of 40 years was well within the agreed-on cost-benefit limits.

The marked decrease in deaths that accompanies mammographic screening has been a major advance for women's health. This is a remarkable achievement, and now, the USPSTF, deciding that women should be allowed to die from their breast cancers, is trying to turn back the clock 20 years. . . . Women should be informed of the "harms" of screening, but they should be provided a clear explanation of the proven benefits so that they can make "informed decisions" for themselves.

6

Mammograms Do Not Save Lives

Veneta Masson

Veneta Masson is an author. Her books and poetry have largely been inspired by her 35 years as a family nurse practitioner spent primarily in the inner city of Washington, DC. Her poetry collections include Rehab at the Florida Avenue Grill *and* Clinician's Guide to the Soul. *Her book* Ninth Street Notebook—Voice of a Nurse in the City *won the 2001 Book of the Year award from the* American Journal of Nursing.

Despite what many health professionals tell their patients and the message the media highlights, mammograms do not save lives. Studies do not show that women who undergo regular screening for breast cancer live any longer than women who are not screened. According to an analysis by an international and independent research center, one woman will benefit for every 2,000 women who are screened regularly for ten years. However, many more women will unnecessarily undergo chemotherapy, radiotherapy, or have their breast removed. Many more women will experience psychological stress from a false-positive result. The US Preventive Services Task Force recommendations advocating that women aged 50 and younger talk to their doctor about screening and that women 50 to 74 be screened every two years, are reasonable.

I knew I had a bladder infection. I knew it because I'd worked as a nurse practitioner for twenty years and had heard the symptoms described hundreds of times. But I wasn't in practice now, and I couldn't verify my own diagnosis or ask a colleague to prescribe antibiotic treatment. Nor had I found another source of primary care for myself. What to do? I remembered that a nurse practitioner I knew slightly had opened a practice within a mile of my house. Perfect. I grabbed the first appointment I could get.

In her office, I filled out a comprehensive health history, deposited a urine sample in a cup, and waited for what I hoped would be a swift and straightforward consultation. But no, my nurse practitioner wanted to talk about my health in general.

"When was your last mammogram?" she asked, scanning the form I'd filled out.

"Two years ago, I think. But I've decided not to do them anymore."

Silence.

"I don't believe they save lives," I added defensively.

I could no longer endorse the tests as routine screening measures for me or any other woman.

Her eyes dropped from my face to my family health history, then moved back up to me.

"Ah, I understand," she said compassionately. "Your sister died of breast cancer and you're still dealing with that." She went on for a while, using words like *anger* and *fear*.

"No," I resisted. "I don't believe early detection guarantees successful treatment or extends life."

"I understand," she consoled me. "You're not ready. But you really need to start getting your mammograms again. Your sister's cancer puts you at higher risk."

I left the office with the prescription I needed and recovered quickly from the bladder infection, but I couldn't put the encounter out of my mind. I thought of all the things I wished I'd been able to say to my colleague. Maybe this: You're wrong about the anger and fear. My sister's cancer, discovered in her early forties during the course of a routine physical exam, sent me deep into the medical literature with an insatiable hunger for information. It's this search for answers and twenty years of experience caring for women—many of whom bore physical or emotional scars acquired in the aftermath of suspicious or inconclusive mammograms—that led me to decide that I could no longer endorse the tests as routine screening measures for me or any other woman.

Slipping Confidence in Screening

At age fifty-six, as I stood in the small room at the breast center, my left breast sandwiched between two metal plates for my yearly mammogram, I didn't realize it would be my last screening. In fact, I can't remember just when my confidence in screening mammograms started to slip. Maybe it was after reading an early edition of *Susan Love's Breast Book*, which I'd bought with the intention of passing it on to my sister the year she had her mastectomy.

I was impressed by how plainly and intelligently Love, a breast surgeon, presented the research findings about mammography. Her discussion of both the pros and cons of routine screening seemed more reasoned than what I was reading in the clinical literature and hearing at conferences. If my physician or nurse practitioner colleagues had reservations about the screening protocols we advocated, they weren't voicing them. Mammograms were, after all, standard practice.

I began to plow through research studies online and in the medical library. I studied the wordings of my patients' and my own mammogram results. They were almost never reported as normal, but as "benign findings" or "no evidence of malignancy at this time." Keep coming back, they seemed to predict, and we'll find it. I observed how the need for a repeated image, a call back, or the mere mention of words like *lump, mass, referral*—even *watch* culled a woman from the world of the carefree well forever.

In my practice and personal life, I saw how women embraced the well-intentioned but relentless messages from medical, workplace, and women's groups to "take the test, not the chance." Mammograms save lives, we were reminded. You owe it to yourself and your family. Be responsible.

Campaigns were mounted against insurers that didn't cover yearly mammograms. Free testing for poor or uninsured women became a cause to be championed. It did no good to remind women that heart disease and lung cancer take more women's lives than breast cancer. They knew that breast cancer strikes younger and harder. And there's no practical way to prevent it.

There were feature stories about celebrity survivors as well as "everyday" women whose breast cancer, thanks to a routine mammogram, was found early and treated fast. Breast cancer gave new meaning to the now-annual race, the color pink, the month of October (which has become Breast Cancer Awareness Month). Industries from T-shirt manufacturers to radiology departments geared up to support this new movement.

The whole engine of breast cancer awareness was—and still is—simply too big, too powerful, and too well funded to gear down.

Then research reports began to filter into the media from unfamiliar, foreign-sounding organizations like the Nordic Cochrane Centre. (The Nordic Cochrane Centre describes itself as "an independent research and information centre that is part of The Cochrane Collaboration, an international network of individuals and institutions committed to preparing, maintaining, and disseminating systematic reviews of the effects of health care" ...) The reports verified the benefit of mammography screening—for a few women, at a significant cost in unnecessary follow-up and treatment for hundreds of others. But minds that were made up didn't open to take in this new information. The whole engine of breast cancer awareness was—and still is—simply too big, too powerful, and too well funded to gear down.

Compelling Data

I continue to shock friends when the subject of their latest date with the mammographer comes up, and I admit that I'm no longer a member of the club. I can't bring myself to smile at the cartoons, laugh at the jokes, forward the e-mails with the funny stories, or wear the pink ribbon. Nor do I, unless asked, elaborate on the compelling data that have informed my own decision.

I discovered early on that facts alone would sway no one. So I simply listen respectfully to other women, many of them close friends. They tell me that, thanks to early detection and surgery—often followed by grueling courses of chemo and radiation—they or their best friend, sister, or mother are here today as survivors with many healthy years ahead of them.

It has not been shown that women who undergo regular screening live longer than those who don't.

They do not question their logic. That is, they don't consider whether the outcome would have been any different without early detection or extensive treatment. And if the many healthy years do not materialize, it is seldom remarked on. The sad truth is that, despite excruciatingly slow advances in treatment, there is still no way of knowing with certainty whether the surgery, chemo, or radiation "got it all."

These days, on the rare occasions when someone really wants to know why I don't get mammograms, I'm glad to be able to share the information from a useful little pamphlet published online in eleven languages in 2008 by that remote-sounding Nordic Cochrane Centre. It's located, as it happens, in Denmark:

> "If 2,000 women are screened regularly for ten years, one will benefit from the screening, as she will avoid dying from breast cancer. At the same time, ten healthy women will- . . . become cancer patients and will be treated unnecessarily. These women will have either a part of their breast or the whole breast removed, and they will often receive radiotherapy, and sometimes chemotherapy. Furthermore, about 200 healthy women will experience a false alarm. The psychological strain until one knows whether or not it was cancer, and even afterward, can be severe."

Another important fact from my friends at the Nordic Cochrane Centre: It has not been shown that women who undergo regular screening live longer than those who don't. This information is available elsewhere in different forms, but I like the clarity and concision of the Nordic Cochrane Centre pamphlet—as well as its list of solid scientific references.

Although I'm fully persuaded, I'm not naïve. I know it will take more than this information for many of my friends to shift their thinking. The "routine" mammogram has become part of the cycle of their year. They get prodding and support from their family, social networks, and doctors who must adhere to community standards of practice. Doctors and other providers, meanwhile, have to reckon with the knowledge that preventive health screening statistics might be collected from patients' charts by review boards, insurers, or plaintiffs' attorneys.

Discord in the Ranks

The *Washington Post* headline late in 2009, "Fierce Debate Raging over New Cancer Test Guidelines," came as no surprise to me. The US Preventive Services Task Force had recommended that women age fifty or younger, as well as those over seventy-five, *talk to their doctor* about how often they should be screened, rather than automatically opting for an annual mammogram. What's more, the task force recommended a screening mammogram every two years for women ages 50–74. The task force is an independent panel of private-sector experts in prevention and primary care; it is currently composed of ten physicians, one nurse, and a Ph.D. in health management and policy. The members had relied on the available evidence, statistical models, and their own professional judgment to reach their conclusions. . . . After the recommendations were released and a heated debate began, the disappointing news that government officials were quick to backpedal from the task force's recommendations didn't surprise me, either.

What? No more yearly mammograms? No routine screening for most women below fifty? The media were quick to highlight the discord among medical professionals who responded publicly to the recommendations.

Some activists suggested that the recommendations were a political move aimed at cutting costs, and that the government and private insurers would soon limit the number of mammograms they would pay for. Those breast cancer awareness advocates who believe that catching cancer early is a matter of life and death cried foul.

Breast care centers with enormous investments in mammography machines and technicians continued to promote the benefits of annual screening. The general public, including most health professionals, clung to the belief that early detection saves lives. They are heavily influenced by vociferous groups and experts with a stake in perpetuating the status quo.

If you are the one in two thousand whose life is extended, that's all that counts.

If you are somehow harmed as a result of annual mammograms, that's the price you pay for access to a test that is considered the "gold standard" in breast cancer detection.

My Perspective

Because I understand that the clinical debate about screening mammograms is far from settled, I'd like to share my own perspective and action plan in the hope that, over time, a new consensus will be reached.

Metastatic breast cancer is terrible, no question. But I agree with the writers of the commentary in the January 13, 2010, issue of the *Journal of the American Medical Association* that breast cancer is just as treatable and just as deadly regardless of screening. I've opted out of routine screening.

I might accept the statistical evidence that because I have a first-degree relative who had breast cancer, my own risk is increased, perhaps even doubled. But that fact doesn't make screening any more valuable to me than it would be to another woman—unless I believe that early detection will guarantee a better outcome for me. I don't.

I've made sure that my primary care physician accepts my reasoning and supports me in my choice, although I welcome information from him about new findings that might affect my decision.

I don't do breast self-exams. There's no evidence to support their effectiveness. But that's not to say I don't pay attention to my body. If I should happen to discover a lump in my breast, I'll have it evaluated. I'm not opposed to having a diagnostic mammogram.

If I'm told a lump is cancerous, I'll seek other opinions. The interpretation of cell changes can be subjective. I want two—or three—expert pathologists to concur on any changes in mine. In July 2010, a *New York Times* article titled "Prone to Error: Earliest Steps to Find Cancer" reported that there is often "outright error" in diagnosing breast cancer in its earliest stages, leading to unnecessary surgery, radiation, and drug treatment—as well as fear—for some women.

I won't rush into treatment because I know that cancers don't develop or spread overnight. Any cancerous lump I find has probably been growing for years. Of course I understand that there are exceptions.

If there are research breakthroughs that dramatically increase the value of early detection, I'll rejoice and change my attitude toward screening accordingly.

It's been ten years since my last mammogram. I don't have to wonder whether this will be the year for a false alarm, false reassurance, or discovery of a cancer that might or might not require treatment.

I accept that sooner or later, I'll die of something. It could be breast cancer. It's also possible that I'll die with cancerous changes in my breast (or some other location) that never progressed enough to cause harm.

I won't think less of any woman who continues to get screening mammograms. The weight of public and professional opinion is still on her side.

It's been ten years since my last mammogram. I don't have to wonder whether this will be the year for a false alarm, false reassurance, or discovery of a cancer that might or might not require treatment. I accept the fact that life is uncertain.

I'm grateful for the gift of good health, recognizing that that's what it is: a gift. I will always mourn my sister's untimely death, which took place three years after her diagnosis despite state-of-the-art treatment. If it were in my power, I'd honor her by redirecting the $5 billion this country spends each year on screening mammography to other purposes. I'd direct those sums instead to the study of how breast cancer starts, and what we can do to treat it more effectively.

7

Lifestyle and Spirituality Are Important for Treating Cancer

Deborah A. Ray

Deborah A. Ray is an advocate for holistic and natural health. She hosts a satellite radio show called Healthy, Wealthy and Wise Health Talk. *She is Vice President of the Alliance for Natural Health (ANH) USA, an organization dedicated to promoting sustainable health and freedom of choice in healthcare. Ray authors a blog on ANH's website.*

Patient lifestyle and spirituality are important but often neglected factors in cancer treatment. Doctors are slowly realizing that aggressive medical treatments to fight cancer, such as chemotherapy and surgery, do not always lead to better outcomes. However, the medical community generally still fails to communicate to cancer patients the significant benefits provided by exercise, a healthy diet, spirituality, and homeopathic remedies. These lifestyle factors can provide significant and sometimes dramatic benefits for people battling cancer.

Cancer care in the U.S. has increasingly become the perfect example that confounds the American mind-set. After all, we have been culturally conditioned that if a little is good, a lot is better, and a whole lot is best of all. Our current American medical system is a great example that more medicine is not necessarily better medicine and often does not translate to a better outcome. And, lest we forget, more expensive care does not always translate into better care. It is becoming increasingly clear that working smarter is very important to navigate the medical system and to insure a better outcome.

Allow me to state my bias up front. In the last year, a dear friend, a close acquaintance, and my husband have all faced cancer. Facing cancer is scary. It completely overwhelms your life. Every day is a new challenge, another doctor with whom to deal, another blood test, another injection, another challenge in nutrition, and every single person who faces cancer is a true hero. You may be scared to death but you are a hero to go through facing cancer in the American medical system. There is no guide; finding your way is a maze. Taking steps to optimize your diet and nutrition, use supplements wisely, address your emotional and spiritual health along with researching and considering treatment options is dizzyingly complex. There are wonderful doctors out there and caring nurses but you are sadly mistaken to think anyone looks at you, your diagnosis, and your lifestyle as a whole. The medical system is much too fragmented for that to occur.

Questioning the Virtues of Conventional Treatments

In December a routine PET scan (part of a follow up program) revealed positive findings and a diagnosis of stage III Lymphoma for my husband. We wondered out loud with his radiation oncologist (who was totally supportive of an integrative approach to a bout of stage I non-aggressive lymphoma 3 years previously) what else could have been done in the subsequent 3 years. We had addressed diet, inflammation, supplementation, hormonal balance, exercise, emotional and spiritual health issues. Was there something we had missed to be facing a serious stage III aggressive form of lymphoma? All the experts we consulted were unanimous that treating the original cancer more aggressively was not an effective way to prevent another bout of cancer. After reading and re-reading

The Emperor of All Maladies, a biography of cancer by Dr. Siddhartha Mukherjee, I became educated that the cancer profession grudgingly came to agreement that more chemo does not necessarily produce a better outcome after years of patient trials and clinical experience. The side effects of additional aggressive chemo invariably outweigh the benefits. Much progress has been made to manage the side effects of chemotherapy. While multiple powerful chemotherapy agents are now the standard of care for many cancer diagnoses, the oncologist was clear "We'll consider 6–8 rounds of chemotherapy, testing you after the initial 4. After 8 treatments, the side effects outweigh any potential benefit."

Even the newer, more expensive drugs are not necessarily better to treat cancer. Gleevec, a new and expensive cancer drug, was acclaimed as a breakthrough for certain leukemia diagnoses yet it is now appreciated that many patients become resistant to its effects. Avastin engendered controversy when federal regulators questioned its price and its success in certain cancer diagnoses. The use of Taxol and Herceptin while once acclaimed is now questioned in many because of the little life gained, their side effects, and their expense.

The same has become true of surgery to address cancer. The initial work of German surgeon Dr. Richard von Volkmann inspired the work of Johns Hopkins professor of surgery, Dr. Richard Halsted. Dr. Halsted and his protégés pioneered and established radical surgery when the patient faced breast cancer as the standard of care. It took many years and many disfigured patients before it was determined that radical, disfiguring surgery did not produce the best outcome for breast cancer. Pioneers like British Dr. Keynes, Dr. Criles, Jr. in the U.S. and Philadelphia surgeon Dr. Fisher along with the subtle shift of the doctor-patient relationship were instrumental for medicine to replace radical disfiguring mastectomies with removal of pectoral muscles and all area lymph glands with lumpectomies and other treatments. The February 8,

2011 issue of *Journal of the American Medical Association* again turned the conventional wisdom of breast cancer surgery inside out. For many patients facing breast cancer at an early stage (estimated to be up to 40,000 per year) the removal of area lymph modes with all of the accompanying side effects is now known to be unnecessary. And, thanks to the Internet (the ultimate lay home medical journal) nearly every woman facing this situation will put this game changer to her surgeon.

Spiritual health and your piece of mind are more important than any cancer treatment, conventional, alternative, or integrative, any diet, or any supplement you may use.

Gilbert Welch, MD, professor of medicine at Dartmouth University and author of *Should I be Tested for Cancer: Maybe Not and Here's Why*, stumped the morning TV talk show hosts with analysis of the medical literature. Mass screening of cancer often does not cause people to live longer or live better. Only those who have a genetic predisposition to cancer or whose environment/lifestyle puts them at risk of cancer are well served by routine cancer screening. The catch it in time mentality sold to all Americans thanks to public service announcements from drug companies and medical device companies has no science to back it up. Screening often identifies abnormalities that are not malignant. Screening can also set the stage for little attention to be paid to one's lifestyle. That alone can be problematic as we now learn that we can turn off and turn on genes with lifestyle choices even innocuous things like laughter. Certainly, environmental factors can be powerful and the sea of chemicals in which we now live and raise our children has been linked to an increased incidence of cancer.

Lack of Awareness About Lifestyle Choices

There is one mention in the 550 page+ *"The Emperor of All Maladies"* of diet, nutrition, and lifestyle. It is a brilliantly written and well documented book. The lack of nutritional and lifestyle focus, research, education of physicians and their medical staff, and what happens in medical offices clearly bears this situation out. Every cancer expert we visited had a bowl of candy in their waiting room. . . . Nearly every oncologist acknowledged to us they knew nothing about diet and cancer. This situation is outrageously insulting to patients. Every parent knows unlimited candy/processed sugar is not good for growing children. Why would candy be acceptable in the office of every cancer treatment facility in the area?

I researched every site, journal, book I could find for my husband's specific diagnosis.

None of these resources mentioned the nuggets we gleamed from phone consultations we scheduled with leading experts in integrative cancer care including:

Spiritual health and your peace of mind are more important than any cancer treatment, conventional, alternative, or integrative, any diet, or any supplement you may use. The support of your respective faith community is amazing and does make a difference.

Exercise is the one thing you can do to reduce your chance of cancer returning by up to 50%. There is no pill with that rate of efficacy.

Diet does matter. Your immune system is 100% protein. It is important to get sufficient amounts (generally 1 g [gram] of protein for every 2 pounds of body weight) of high quality protein along with a nutrient dense diet focusing on fruits and vegetables. When your appetite fails and your GI tract is queasy, it is important to focus on foods that pack a nutritional punch. Good fats with their ability to modulate inflammation make a big difference, too. Take the bad fats out of your diet; if you eat a grain make it a whole grain; eat up to

11 servings of fruits and vegetables a day; eat some good fats each day; and get adequate protein. Sugar with its ability to stun the infection fighting white blood cells is not recommended for any cancer patient.

There are some amazing foods/nutrients specific for certain cancers and certain chemo agents that our experts shared with us. I found none of these even with research skills honed from 26 years on air. . . . Sun Soup (mushrooms, Chinese herbs, certain vegetables) has an amazing ability to prolong the life of certain lung cancer patients. Cinnamon and Lemon Grass are worth considering for lymphoma. A blend of Ayurvedic/Indian herbs, Amrit Kalash, has good science about its benefits when used by those taking chemotherapy. . . . The use of plantain extract has been studied in a major cancer center and can be used topically to diminish the side effects of radiation. Intravenous vitamin C has been studied at NIH [National Institutes of Health], University of KS [Kansas], and other centers with positive results.

Knowing Where to Look

There is so much more that no one tells you but is in the scientific literature if you know the places to look or who to ask.

Homeopathy may well be an unsung remedy of choice for many. The National Cancer Institute, MD Anderson Cancer Center, Memorial Sloan Kettering Cancer Center, and others are looking seriously at the work of doctors using homeopathic remedies in foundations in India. The success rate can be impressive. At the least, there are ways to deal with the side effects of conventional cancer care (chemotherapy and radiation) using homeopathic remedies that are very successful. For example, there are various drug injections or blood transfusions used when chemotherapy invariably suppresses the bone marrows production of blood cells. These can adversely affect how long you live and can cause other side effects including all your bones aching. There is a homeopathic remedy, Ferrum phos, along with acupuncture that work quite well without these downsides and side effects. Who knew??

There are therapies widely used in Europe and other countries that are never mentioned to most U.S. patients. The use of sound and light (photo and sonodynamic therapy) for certain cancer diagnoses is very real in other countries but not the U.S. Most European oncologists offer Coley's fluid, once used routinely in the U.S., to harness the body's power of fever and immune response to treat cancer. European cancer clinics use heat (hyperthermia) to treat cancer much more gently than chemotherapy and radiation and while it is being studied at a major U.S. university, most oncologists never mention it to their patients. Worse yet, in the year 2011 patients continue to be pressured using tactics that are not professional when they choose to go a route outside surgery, chemotherapy, and radiation.

It appears to be up to patients to educate themselves about the fact that lifestyle does matter.

Medicine has no explanation for patients who beat the odds, exceptional patients or spontaneous remissions. There is no medical certainty with regards to who survives, who does not, and for how long. Every patient is an individual with a personal genetic map in a unique environment affected by physical, emotional, and spiritual factors exclusive to them. Statistics are just numbers on a piece of paper. Hope conquers all is not a cliché. Faith that sustains you can be as real as anything injected into you or given to you orally.

Patients have forever changed the practice of cancer medicine. It appears to be up to patients to educate themselves about the fact that lifestyle does matter. Lifestyle choices may actually affect how genes express themselves and whether cancer ever develops. Lifestyle choices undoubtedly affect how well those do when faced with cancer.

8

Artificial Intelligence Can Help Find a Cure for Cancer

Jay M. Tenenbaum and Jeff Shrager

Jay M. Tenenbaum is a fellow at the American Association for Artificial Intelligence and is a consulting professor of Information Technology at Carnegie Mellon's West Coast campus. Jeff Shrager is a computational psychologist of science and a consulting associate professor at Stanford University. Tenenbaum and Shrager are founders of the company CollabRx.

Artificial Intelligence (AI) is a powerful tool that can be used to find a cure for cancer. Physicians and scientists have realized that cancer is not a single disease. Every patient's cancer tumor is unique. Doctors hold a wealth of information about how each of the unique cancer tumors they treat responds to different drug treatments. However, this information is generally lost because it is not shared, organized, or expanded. Cancer Commons, a web-based application that is based on AI, can tap into this lost information, organize it and make it available to other doctors. In the short term, AI can help individual cancer patients survive, and someday in the future possibly even cure cancer.

Despite enormous strides in scientific understanding and medical treatment, cancer still kills millions of people each year. This article will explore why cancer has proven to be such a formidable adversary, and how AI [Artificial Intelligence] and machine learning (ML) can save lives by helping individual patients beat the odds.

Jay M. Tenenbaum and Jeff Shrager, "Cancer: A Computational Disease That AI Can Cure," *AI Magazine*, Summer 2011. Copyright © 2011, Association for the Advancement of Artificial Intelligence. All rights reserved. Reproduced with permission.

Modern molecular biology supports the hypothesis that cancer is actually hundreds or thousands of rare diseases, and that every patient's tumor is, to some extent, unique. Although there is a rapidly growing arsenal of targeted cancer therapies that can be highly effective in specific subpopulations, especially when used in rational combinations to block complementary pathways, the pharmaceutical industry continues to rely on large-scale randomized clinical trials that test drugs individually in heterogeneous populations. Such trials are an extremely inefficient strategy for searching the combinational treatment space, and capture only a small portion of the data needed to predict individual treatment responses. On the other hand, an estimated 70 percent of all cancer drugs are used off label in cocktails based on each individual physician's experience, as if the nation's 30,000 oncologists are engaged in a gigantic uncontrolled and unobserved experiment, involving hundreds of thousands of patients suffering from an undetermined number of diseases. These informal experiments could provide the basis for what amounts to a giant adaptive search for better treatments, if only the genomic and outcomes data could be captured and analyzed, and the findings integrated and disseminated.

Toward this end we are developing Cancer Commons, a family of web-based rapid-learning communities in which physicians, patients, and scientists collaborate to individualize cancer therapy. The goals of this initiative are to (1) give each patient the best possible outcome by individualizing his or her treatment based on their tumor's genomic subtype, (2) learn as much as possible from each patient's response, and (3) rapidly disseminate what is learned. The key innovation is to run this adaptive search strategy in "real time," so that the knowledge learned from one patient is disseminated in time to help the next.

Cancer Commons provides an exciting and important domain for the application of AI and ML. Achieving its goals will require developing models for predicting individual responses to cancer therapies and using them to plan and run thousands of adaptive treatment experiments. The genomic and clinical response data from each patient can be analyzed to continuously improve the predictive models, as well as our understanding of cancer biology and drugs. Each patient is treated in accord with the best available knowledge, and that knowledge is continually updated to benefit the next patient.

It is unlikely that a single cure will be found for cancer—it is not a single disease.

In the next section, we review the current paradigm for translational cancer research, and its limitations, as we enter the new era of genomics and personalized medicine. Then we introduce Cancer Commons as a new, open-science paradigm for real-time translational research. . . .

Cancer Research in the Era of Genomics and Personalized Medicine

It is unlikely that a single cure will be found for cancer—it is not a single disease. To a first approximation, cancer is what happens when a normal cell mutates in such a way that it can reproduce but no longer control its growth. As genome sequencing becomes less expensive and more widespread, scientists are finding a spectacular variety of mutations that lead to cancerous growth. Consensus is building that, because cancer is an individualized disease, it must be addressed through individualized treatment.

Developing and justifying individualized cancer treatments is a very difficult problem. First, each organ-specific cancer involves many rare genomic alterations, thus leading to highly heterogeneous disease populations. This heterogeneity flows directly from the underlying biological and genetic complexity of cancer. The mutation history of each tumor cell is also unique—the result of cascading and compounding errors in the cell's machinery for maintaining the integrity of its DNA, as well as evolutionary adaptations that help it evade therapy.

Genetic mutations typically manifest themselves through cell signaling pathways, chains of protein-catalyzed reactions that govern basic cellular functions such as cell division, cell movement, how a cell responds to specific external stimuli, and even cell death. The proteins in a pathway often communicate by adding phosphate groups, which act as "on" or "off" switches, to a neighboring protein. When one of the oncogenes [cancer genes] that codes for such proteins is mutated, the resulting protein can be stuck in the "on" or "off" position, leading to uncontrolled cell growth, and thus cancer.

In contrast to traditional chemotherapy, which targets all rapid cell growth, modern targeted cancer therapies attempt to block specific molecules in the signaling pathways. Targeted therapies may be more effective than current treatments and less harmful to normal cells. However, a given patient may require a custom cocktail of targeted therapies to block both the pathways directly affected by an oncogene as well as secondary pathways that may enable the cell to evade therapy.

Large-scale clinical trials are problematic in genomic diseases like cancer because they rely on population statistics rather than individual responses. A drug that works on 50 percent of patients tested may or may not be better for any given patient than one that works on 20 percent. This inability to account for individual responses may explain why so many late-stage trials fail to demonstrate statistical efficacy, even though a few individuals do respond. What disease did these responders have, that used to be called "breast cancer" or "melanoma," for which there is now an effective drug? How many other cancer patients have the same genomic disease? Unfortunately, we'll never know because when a trial fails, the drug is, as a rule, abandoned.

One happy exception to this rule involves Gleevec (Imatinib), originally developed in 1998 by Novartis for chronic myelogenous leukemia (CML). Gleevec was among the first of a new generation of targeted therapies developed to block a specific enzyme—in this case, BCR-ABL—in a cancer signaling pathway. Shortly after its development, it was experimentally observed that Gleevec also blocked a structurally similar enzyme called c-KIT, which was a primary cause of gastrointestinal stromal tumors (GISTs), a rare form of sarcoma. Gleevec was subsequently tested on many forms of cancer, including a 2003 trial for melanoma that failed. There were, however, a handful of responders in that trial, all of whom had two things in common: their primary tumors were located not on their skin, but in places where the sun don't shine (for example inside the mouth), and their tumors all had a mutated c-KIT gene. In 2008, results of a definitive trial testing Gleevec on patients whose tumors had been pretested for c-KIT mutations demonstrated a major response. A randomized trial would have needed perhaps a million patients to demonstrate statistical significance for a drug that affected at most 3 percent of melanoma patients. There's more to this story, and we'll return to it several times.

We need a smarter way to search for effective treatments.

As we enter the age of personalized genomic medicine, the Gleevec experience will become the norm. At the molecular level, cancer is hundreds if not thousands of unique diseases. Given that there are more than 800 therapies in development targeting specific mutations, and that they will often have to be used together in cocktails to ensure a durable response, there simply isn't enough time, money, patients, or specimens to test treatments individually on large heterogeneous patient populations. We need a smarter way to search for effective treatments, one that utilizes the complete molecular and clinical profile of every patient to efficiently decide which drugs are likely to work best in a specific patient.

Community oncology practices, where the vast majority of patients are treated, provide a promising way forward. Every day, thousands of patients who have exhausted the standard of care are treated with off-label drugs and cocktails. These treatment decisions are based largely on the judgments and experience of individual physicians, and the results are seldom reported. What if we could coordinate these thousands of ad hoc "N of 1" experiments, capture their results, and integrate them with the evidence from large-scale controlled trials? Cancer Commons provides the platform for doing just that, transforming the everyday practice of oncology into a giant adaptive search for better treatments.

Cancer Commons

Cancer Commons is a family of web-based rapid learning communities where physicians, scientists, and patients collaborate to individualize therapies based on the molecular profile of each tumor. Cancer Commons provides physicians with the knowledge and resources to treat each patient in the best possible way, and to disseminate the resulting data and knowledge as efficiently as possible to help subsequent patients. Cancer Commons is, in essence, a huge adaptive clinical trial, whose goal is to continuously improve patient outcomes, rather than to demonstrate the efficacy of a specific drug for regulatory approval.

Cancer Commons is being developed one cancer at a time, beginning with melanoma. At the core of each Commons is a molecular disease model (MDM). MDMs are expert-curated reference models enumerating the known molecular subtypes of a cancer. Each subtype is linked to relevant pathways, diagnostic tests, approved and experimental (targeted) therapies, and clinical trials. At each point in time, oncologists can use the appropriate MDM to treat patients with the best available therapies for their tumors' molecular subtype. The subtypes and associated therapies can be continually refined based on how patients respond. For example, subtypes can be split corresponding to responders and nonresponders, and new subtypes added to accommodate previously unseen tumor types. Conceptually, all patients within Cancer Commons are participating in a huge, continuously running, adaptive clinical trial that is constantly testing and refining both the MDM subtypes and their potential treatments.

The power in the Cancer Commons approach lies in the rapid feedback loop that is generated when a patient is rationally treated based on his or her molecular subtype but does not respond as predicted. Armed with state of the art genomics technology, researchers can attempt to uncover why that individual failed to respond and apply the findings to the next patient with the same molecular subtype. Studying response outliers can be particularly informative. Earlier, we discussed the example of a handful of melanoma patients who responded to Gleevec in a trial that failed to meet its clinical end points. The flip side is the subset of patients who fail to respond in a successful trial. For those patients that were directed to the trial through Cancer Commons, one can go back to the scientists on whose research the molecular disease model was based and ask them to revise the model based on the new molecular and clinical data from the subset of nonresponding patients. What disease subtype did they have and how should it be treated? These questions are not academic; they pertain to patients who urgently need new options. Over time, the answers should lead to MDM models with increasingly specific molecular subclasses, linked to increasingly efficacious therapies.

Cancer Commons' rapid learning loop . . . applies the same continuous improvement philosophy to drug development and clinical trials that management gurus like W. Edwards Deming used in the 1980s and 1990s to slash time and costs in automobile manufacturing and many other industries. It is also related to the concept that Andy Grove, the former CEO of Intel, had in mind when he advocated, in an influential *JAMA* [*Journal of the American Medical Association*] editorial, that the pharmaceutical industry should strive to achieve the fast "knowledge turns" achieved by chipmakers. According to *The Economist*, "A knowledge turn [. . .] is the time it takes for an experiment to proceed from hypothesis to results, and then to a new hypothesis—around 18 months in chipmaking, but 10–20 years in medicine."

From an AI perspective, finding effective treatments for cancer is a very high-dimensionality search problem, guided by our rapidly increasing knowledge of cancer biology and drugs.

In addition to accelerating clinical research, Cancer Commons also accelerates communication of the results and subsequent collaborations. The MDMs serve as living review articles, maintained online and continuously updated by top cancer experts. Clinicians and researchers can post peer-reviewed clinical observations and data, anecdotal case reports, rational treatment hypotheses, and actionable research findings to the relevant MDM subtype—preliminary results that are too early for formal presentation in journals or at conferences but that may be helpful to late-stage patients running out of options. Physicians and patients who choose to act on these postings can then report clinical outcomes and side effects from their "N of 1" experiments through the web. Treatment hypotheses that prove successful in a few patients can be generalized to a specific molecular phenotype and validated in proof-of-concept studies or small clinical trials. Hypotheses that hold up can ultimately be incorporated into the guidelines as the new standard of care. Hypotheses and observations that don't hold up can be quickly rejected or revised based on the data points from human subjects. . . .

AI Opportunities and Challenges

From an AI perspective, finding effective treatments for cancer is a very high-dimensionality search problem, guided by our rapidly increasing knowledge of cancer biology and drugs. The number of potential hypotheses about the causes and associated treatments of the disease is huge, especially when complete genomic profiles and combinational therapies are considered—exponentially larger than the number of patients that could represent each possible combination of factors. It is therefore essential to use knowledge to focus the search on promising opportunities, learn as much as possible from every patient, and generalize that knowledge to benefit future patients.

Cancer Commons is an ideal framework for creating human-machine knowledge systems to efficiently conduct this search for better treatments. Think of the networked MDMs as a web-based blackboard and the apps as knowledge sources. The MDMs organize the world's knowledge about cancer subtypes, pathways, tests, drugs, and trials, and that knowledge is made available in a semantic web-compatible format. The human-machine knowledge system that is Cancer Commons generates and tests hypotheses, creates plans, and learns. This shared human-machine approach is essential because although the complexity of the search demands computational management, it is ultimately human medical specialists who interact with patients and who are responsible for carrying out treatment plans. It is imperative that the physicians and patients understand the general rationale behind all decisions and inferences. . . .

Cancer Commons is the harbinger of a new patient-centered paradigm for cancer research in which every patient receives individualized therapy based upon the best available knowledge and where the resulting data contributes as efficiently as possible to improved treatment for each subsequent patient. AI and machine learning will be essential to realizing this vision.

While AI may not be able to cure cancer any time soon, it may soon make life or death differences in outcomes for individual patients.

Cancer, as a domain, presents the AI and ML communities with extraordinary challenges and, hence, opportunities. These include (1) managing the sheer quantity and heterogeneity of the data and knowledge involved—encompassing millions of medical records, genomewide datasets, and documents; (2) planning thousands of complex, multistep treatment strategies that ethically balance the needs of the individual with those of science; (3) capturing and analyzing the results of these treatment experiments in diverse causal and empirical models of cancer biology and drug response; (4) continuously testing and refining these models to account for new clinical and laboratory findings; (5) generalizing the models across patients and cancers and integrating them to improve decision making; and (6) integrating human and machine planning, learning, and decision making to exploit their respective strengths.

Taken together, these challenges add up to the grand challenge of curing cancer. This challenge is a worthy heir to the succession of grand challenges—from chess to unmanned vehicles—that have driven so much progress in AI over the years. While AI may not be able to cure cancer any time soon, it may soon make life or death differences in outcomes for individual patients.

9

Cancer Will Likely Become A Chronic, Manageable Disease

David Godkin

David Godkin is a science and medical writer. His work has appeared in Scientific American, Medical Post, *and many other publications in the US and Canada. He won the 2003 Canadian Science Writers' Association award for best feature article.* Medical Post *is an independent weekly newspaper for Canadian doctors.*

Most US and Canadian physicians do not think a cure for all cancers will be found in the next few decades. However, most of them do think that science will make significant progress that will lead to many cancers becoming chronic, but manageable diseases. The costs in both human resources and financial resources of treating and managing cancer as a chronic disease will not be insignificant and will require new thinking on the part of the government and the healthcare community.

Cure cancer by 2050? The ramifications of this question are examined in this instalment of the *Medical Post*'s "What if?" series.

Certainly how we understand and treat this disease will have changed by this future date. Instead of referring to breast or prostate cancer, doctors will talk to patients about their mutational profiles, genomic snapshots of breakage at the molecular level that are harbingers of cancer. They'll prescribe drugs similar in effect to Gleevec, which is used to combat abnormal cellular proteins on the tips of patients' chromosomes that lead to chronic myeloid leukemia. They'll discover new ways to keep cancer from recurring.

But cure it?

"I think it is possible to cure cancer," says Dr. Glen Weiss, director of thoracic oncology at the Translational Genomics Research Institute in Phoenix. "We may not get all the cancer types and subtypes initially, but step by step we might find the cure or magic regimen if it's a combination of surgery, chemotherapy and radiation together."

Some cancers, perhaps even many, will be cured. But as for the rest of the cancers out there, there is a growing consensus that they will instead become chronic, manageable diseases.

Others, including Dr. Jean Maroun, a medical oncologist and professor of medicine at the University of Ottawa, are less certain. "It is possible that many of the cancers we deal with today will be cured with treatment, but I wouldn't say that they're all going to be cured because some will continue to be resistant."

Dr. Alice Wei, a surgical oncologist with Toronto's University Health Network, is more emphatic. "I don't think cancer is going to disappear," she says flatly.

At the very least, it seems there is general agreement that some cancers, perhaps even many, will be cured. But as for the rest of the cancers out there, there is a growing consensus that they will instead become chronic, manageable diseases.

The Human Factor

The main goal of medicine is to relieve patient suffering. Some of the most exciting developments on that score are effective, less toxic cancer-fighting drugs, says Dr. Michael Wosnick, vice-president of research for the Canadian Cancer Society. Aided by our understanding of the human genome, researchers are developing agents that target the unique mutational properties of cancer cells, killing those cells while sparing normal ones.

"In real estate the most important thing is location, location, location," says Dr. Wosnick. "Well, the more selective, the more specific you can make the drug, then the milder treatment, the fewer the side-effects, the better the outcome and the patient's quality of life during and after treatment will be preserved."

For Dr. Michel Tremblay, medical oncologist and director of the Rosalind and Morris Goodman Cancer Center in Montreal, the underlying question is how we measure success in treating cancer. Medical oncologists get very excited, for example, when they discover a four-month median survival rate for their patients. Patients facing a barrage of surgical, radiation and chemotherapeutic treatments are less impressed.

"The five-year survival is nice, but on top of that you should have an index of quality of life," Dr. Tremblay says. "If you're five years in bed and you're still kicking, that's not necessarily a good readout. If you're five years working, being with your children, living a productive life—this is a real contribution."

"Survivorship," a relatively new concept in cancer control, envisions the entire field of cancer treatment mobilized around alleviating the broader challenges facing patients. Comorbidity, patient psychology, pressures on the patient's family and problems navigating a complex health-care system together can have a profound impact on a patients quality of life.

"The problem," says Richard Doll, director of the sociobehavioural research centre and provincial leader for cancer rehabilitation at the BC Cancer Agency, "has been that traditionalists have viewed the cancer problem as treating a tumour, and if you treat the tumour successfully you've essentially done your job. Patients are telling us, 'You need to pay attention to us in other ways.'"

Psychosocial interventions for patients and families, and long-term followup, Doll argues, will be vital. But we won't have to wait until 2050 to see the results. As early as 2015, he says, the concept of survivorship will lead to "significant changes in the recognition of supportive care and quality of life interventions as being a crucial part of the cancer management problem."

Human Resources

The Canadian Partnership Against Cancer's (CPAC) stance is unequivocal: A "national strategy" to fight cancer requires a clear understanding of the number of troops you have in the field—and how many you may need in the future. The trouble is, even CPAC's human resources action group can't say precisely what level of human resources is dedicated to cancer, and consequently whether this is enough.

But here's what it can say: In 2009, Canada boasted just more than 400 medical oncologists and 100 surgical oncologists. Radiation therapists number approximately 1,900 (excluding Quebec) and radiation oncologists nearly 400. Of the nearly 262,000 registered nurses in this country in 2008, more than 3,350 worked in oncology. Also, according to a report to be released later this year by the Canadian Cancer Research Alliance, roughly 1,600 researchers were dedicated solely to investigating cancer between 2005 and 2007.

Are these numbers sufficient to meet the needs of cancer research and treatment today? "Everyone feels there is a shortage of medical oncologists," says Dr. Renaud Whittom, president of the Canadian Association of Medical Oncologists.

Most radiation specialists feel the same, adds Dr. Matthew Parliament, president of the Canadian Association of Radiation Oncology. "In many parts of Canada, 35% or less of incident cancer cases currently receive radiotherapy. The reason for this disparity is not completely understood, but probably relates to a lack of appreciation by referring doctors and specialists of the benefits of radiotherapy."

The situation is equally dire in the U.S. A 2007 workforce study by the American Society of Clinical Oncology (ASCO) concluded that American cancer specialists' struggle to handle the patient load will hit crisis levels by 2020, when demand for oncologists is expected to increase by 48% and the number actually working falls by 4,000. The solution, according to Dr. Michael Goldstein, co-chairman of ASCO's workforce advisory group, will be to fill that gap with nurse petitioners.

"While oncologists will continue to provide hands-on patient care, integrating nurse practitioners and physician assistants has significant potential to extend the supply of oncologist services, particularly in the care for the growing number of cancer survivors," says Dr. Goldstein.

CPAC says similar innovative solutions are needed here in Canada—for example, having specially trained nurses perform colorectal screening to free up physicians to focus on patients needing more specialized care. Or creating a patient "navigator" role for nurses to guide patients through the labyrinthine cancer control network, providing them with knowledge and support and troubleshooting any issues or unanticipated delays along the way.

Will all this become moot with the elimination or significant management of cancer in the decades ahead? Don't count on it, says Dr. Parliament. "Paradoxically, the workload of radiation specialists may actually increase, since patients with cancer may live longer and it may be necessary to add radiation to deal with their symptoms."

Some cancers will certainly become more manageable "due to better screening and treatment," says Jennifer Wiernikowski, president of the Canadian Association of Nursing Oncology, "so this nursing specialty will always be needed in some capacity."

Better drug treatments mean "more people will survive a disease and be living with it on an ongoing basis," says Mamie Mitchell, head of the B.C. Pharmacy Association. "So community pharmacists are going to be playing an important role there, too."

Were cancer to be cured or significantly managed as a chronic disease, economies of scale in a society dominated by older people could result in more cancer patients taking charge of their own care.

Ethical Dilemmas

Most understand beneficence and non-maleficence as the instincts to do good and avoid harming the patient. Justice in relation to medicine is a harder concept to understand and even harder to apply.

However, in recent years, the greatest attention has been paid to the principle of autonomy, which centres on the patient's ability to control the decisionmaking process. Were cancer to be cured or significantly managed as a chronic disease, economies of scale in a society dominated by older people could result in more cancer patients taking charge of their own care.

The key is patients being well-informed, says Dr. Jeff Blackmer, executive director of the Canadian Medical Association's office of ethics. "We see that in an illness like HIV/AIDS where you have an extremely informed patient population who are very involved in managing their conditions. I don't think it's wrong to say that cancer is probably headed in that direction as well."

Increasingly, the health-care system is under pressure to provide patients with access to new therapies. The justice—or injustice—that occurs when people are provided or denied access becomes heightened in a system where provinces make therapy evaluations and funding decision independent of one another. Dr. Blackmer calls it a "patchwork approach" to access to new therapies across Canada.

"If you're a 75-year-old lung cancer patient in Saskatchewan, under the Canada Health Act you should have equal access to care and treatment as someone in Manitoba. But based on the way the provinces decide what therapies to fund, that may or may not be true," he says.

Dr. Ruchika Mishra (PhD), a bioethics fellow with the California Pacific Medical Center in San Francisco, says justice requires that people who qualify for treatment be treated regardless of their ability to pay. At the same time, limited resources sometimes may force us to choose in favour of a 29-year-old cancer patient witha potentially long life in front of her over a 65-year-old- despite the fact the latter has worked hard all his life and paid taxes to support the health-care system.

Ethical quandaries like these are compounded by others, says Dr. Mishra. "One also needs to take into account the principle of beneficence to determine who this treatment is going to benefit the most. Who is going to have the maximum chance of survival?"

Our ethical obligations don't end at North American borders. Today, cancer accounts for one in eight deaths globally. More than 70% of all cancer deaths occur in low- and middle-income countries. By 2030, the American Cancer Society estimates that 83% of tobacco related deaths worldwide will occur in these countries.

"Justice on a global level," says Dr. Blackmer, "is of an order of magnitude higher than the considerations on the local level."

Finances

Knowing the precise economic burden of cancer should provide a good argument for why more funding is required for research and treatment. Lamentably, the Canadian Cancer Society relies on a 13-year-old document, "The Economic Burden of Illness in Canada, 1998" to gauge the impact. Apply the cost of living index to the figures contained in that report to last year's costs and the picture becomes a little clearer: Each year, cancer costs Canadians $3.2 billion in direct costs, including $269 million for drugs and $427 million in physician services. (This calculation does not account for population growth or increases in the number of cancer patients.)

The numbers in the U.S., as might be expected, are even higher: approximately $264 billion, including more than $100 billion in direct medical costs and more than $140 billion in lost productivity. Eliminate cancer and you free up those resources to offset the direct costs of other diseases: diabetes, $92 billion; heart disease, $78 billion; and COPD [chronic obstructive pulmonary disease], $31.4 billion.

Some, such as Dr. Otis Brawley, chief medical officer for the American Cancer Society, say we can't wait, that we must find ways to cut cancer costs now. Consider, he says, the gauntlet of chemotherapeutic drugs that patients with non-small cell lung cancer often undergo.

"There is no evidence that giving these third-, fourth- and fifth-line therapies is going to be beneficial to the patient. There is tremendous evidence that they are highly costly. What we should do as physicians is not abandon the idea of treating people with metastatic disease, but try to be more selective in who we treat for metastatic disease."

One of the fastest growing cost areas in cancer is molecular diagnostic testing. According to Dr. Craig Earle, a medical oncologist affiliated with the Ontario Institute for Cancer Research (OICR), research has provided useful tests that predict whether treatments will work; notable among these are tests for the KRAS mutation in colon cancer and HER2 testing in breast cancer. The problem, however, is that these tests are difficult to conduct, and take longer to show response and outcome. That has cost implications.

"Especially in the U.S., there's been a proliferation of tests that are being done and billed for that really only add marginally to what we already know about patients' prognoses based on clinical measures such as disease stage and performance status," says Dr. Earle. "The cost of this, if left unchecked, can be huge."

Dr. David Levy, president of the BC Cancer Agency says better cost control begins with close collaboration between researchers and clinicians to develop protocols that have a practical benefit for patients. The trick is to ensure the protocols are then aligned with public health-care budgets.

As our population ages rapidly in the years ahead, there will be more cancer—and more costs.

"Were building a (breast cancer) protocol that says what's going to happen to the patient. The patient knows what's going to happen. Everyone in the system knows what's going to happen next and we've got agreement with the government to line up the Medical Services Plan so the dollars follow the patient," he says.

Suggestions for more streamlined cost control are dwarfed, however, by one indisputable fact: As our population ages rapidly in the years ahead, there will be more cancer—and more costs. According to a 2006 discussion paper by the Governing Council of the Canadian Strategy for Cancer Control, by 2036 cancer will have gobbled up $177.5 billion in direct health-care costs, reduced taxation revenues by $250 billion and cost the Canadian economy $543 billion in lost wages.

Reversing this trend has its own cost implications: By curing more cancers and managing the rest, people will live longer and need more care—with fewer young people in the work force to pay for that care. . . .

Cancer Control

"Facts are stubborn things," John Adams, the second president of the United States, famously once said, "and whatever may be our wishes, our inclinations or the dictates of our passion, they cannot alter the state of facts and evidence."

Those who battle cancer face their own stubborn facts. The most obdurate of these are the well over 100 distinct types of cancer and a great many more subtypes of tumours that can occur within specific organs.

Genomic science tells us we can kill these cancers by devising new therapies to target the mutations in a patients DNA—easily said until you consider the estimated 180,000 mutations that can occur in the roughly 12,000 genes that make up the human genome.

We need to treat the fight against cancer not as a war, but as "a terrorist insurgency"—battling it not on a single front, but on many fronts.

These stubborn facts lead us to one overriding and indisputable fact: Absent dramatic changes in the prevention, diagnosis and treatment of cancer, the incidence of cancer and cancer deaths will only rise—and with our aging population—rise dramatically.

By 2020, according to the American Cancer Society, the number of new cancer cases worldwide is expected to increase to 16.8 million annually. By 2030, that number will balloon to 27 million, with 17 million cancer deaths.

Wishing it otherwise won't make it so.

Facts like these may explain why more people talk about "cancer control" than about "beating" cancer outright. They explain a growing consensus that what is required is not some "magic bullet" to defeat cancer but a whole new way of thinking about cancer: Far from needing fewer medical professionals once we cure cancer, we'll need more medical professionals to help manage it as a chronic disease.

Managing cancer will require more co-operation and input from patients, who in turn will demand greater attention to their quality of life and to a more just and equitable way of allocating resources in the fight against cancer.

Those resources include money far—more money than the $3.2 billion Canadians currently spend each year on cancer—and more importantly, money that is spent wisely, that follows the patient.

According to the OICR's Dr. Earle, we need to treat the fight against cancer not as a war, but as "a terrorist insurgency"—battling it not on a single front, but on many fronts, relying not a single magic bullet, but on the many weapons at our disposal.

10

Lung Cancer Research Is Underfunded

Onkar Khullar and Yolonda L. Colson

Onkar Khullar and Yolanda L. Colson are on the faculty at Harvard Medical School. Khullar is a Clinical Fellow in Surgery at Beth Israel-Deaconess Medical Center. Colson is an assistant professor of Surgery. She is also an assistant professor of Medicine within Pulmonary and Critical Care Medicine at Brigham and Women's Hospital.

Lung cancer kills more people than any other cancer. However, its share of federal funding for research and prevention are small compared to other cancers. Generous funding levels for breast and prostate cancers have contributed to a significant drop in deaths and an increase in the survival rate for these cancers. However, the death rate and survival rate for lung cancer have remained dismal for many years. It is time to rectify this disparity and provide more funding for the number one cancer killer in America.

Despite major advances in the field of oncology in research, diagnostic methods, and treatment modalities, lung cancer remains the leading cause of cancer death in the United States among both men and women. With an estimated 215,020 new cases and 161,840 deaths in 2008, lung cancer is responsible for more than 25% of all cancer deaths. Given these alarming statistics, one would assume that lung

Onkar Khullar and Yolonda L. Colson, "The Underfunding of Lung Cancer Research," *The Journal of Thoracic and Cardiovascular Surgery*, August 2009. All rights reserved. Reproduced with permission.

cancer research would be a priority for funding. Surprisingly, this could not be further from the truth. In terms of research funding, lung cancer is all but forgotten.

Various government agencies fund cancer research, including the National Institutes of Health (NIH) and National Cancer Institute (NCI), the Department of Defense (DOD), and the Centers for Disease Control and Prevention (CDC). Of the $5.570 billion in NIH funding for all cancer research in 2008, $726 million was granted for breast cancer, $290 million for prostate cancer, and $274 million for colorectal cancer. Unfortunately, only $169 million was spent on research for the number one cancer killer, lung cancer. Similarly, in 2008 the DOD sponsored $138 million to fund breast cancer research, $80 million for prostate cancer, and $10 million for ovarian cancer. Meanwhile, lung cancer was given no designated funding. Fortunately, recent advocacy has resulted in the funding of a new $20-million Lung Cancer Research Program through the DOD for fiscal year 2009. Nonetheless, overall federal research funding per cancer death remains 21 times greater for breast cancer and 13 times greater for prostate cancer than for lung cancer research.

The urgency to obtain more funding for lung cancer research has never been greater, as this disease accounts for more deaths than breast, prostate, colorectal, liver, and ovarian cancers combined.

This alarming disparity is not simply isolated to cancer research funding but also extends to lung cancer prevention and control, where a surprising two thirds of the $300,000 earmarked by the CDC is allocated to breast and cervical cancer while only $100,000 of the CDC budget is focused on smoking cessation. No CDC dollars are earmarked for prevention of lung cancer aside from smoking cessation, and although smoking cessation is extremely important, it is not appropriate to assume that it is the cure for all lung cancer, anymore than it is the cure for all cases of coronary artery disease or stroke. The average person with lung cancer stopped smoking nearly a decade before the development of lung cancer, and the incidence of lung cancer among nonsmokers is estimated to be as high as 30,000 to 50,000 cases/year.

Lack of Funding Has Hindered the Ability to Save Lives

Our point is not that the funding for breast and prostate cancer is undeserved—cancer is a devastating disease, regardless of the location—rather, it is critical to call attention to the disparity in lung cancer funding and its effects on patients with lung cancer. Nowhere is the disparity in the "war against cancer" more obvious than in survival. From 1999 to 2005, the 5-year survival for all cancers combined was 66%: 89% for breast cancer, 99% for prostate cancer, and a dismal 16% for lung cancer. Furthermore, from 1975 to 2005, the 5-year survivals improved by 15% for breast cancer, 30% for prostate cancer, and a mere 3% for lung cancer.

The urgency to obtain more funding for lung cancer research has never been greater, as this disease accounts for more deaths than breast, prostate, colorectal, liver, and ovarian cancers combined. During the past 30 years, there has been minimal improvement in lung cancer mortality. The lack of effective funding for lung cancer research has significantly hindered the ability of researchers to elucidate the pathogenesis behind this disease process and to find effective cures for smokers and nonsmokers alike. Yet lung cancer is not hopeless; we should not abandon these patients. Akin to the advances in breast cancer during the past 35 years, recent identification of specific gene mutations within lung cancers also promises to yield both prognostic and therapeutic benefits, particularly if appropriate research funding is made available. Lung cancer needs to be brought to the forefront of the nation's research agenda and to be supported with representative levels of funding. It is time to address this forgotten malignancy, the number one cancer killer in America, and turn our collective research focus toward a cure for lung cancer.

11

Cancer Research Receives More Funding than Heart Research

Shelley Wood

Shelley Wood is a medical journalist for Heartwire, *an online source of cardiology news. Wood was awarded a National Institute for Health Care Management (NIHCM) Print Journalism Award in 2009.*

Heart disease is the number one killer of Americans. However, cancer research gets more US government funding than heart disease research. Cancer also receives more nonprofit funding than cardiovascular disease. It is not clear why this funding difference exists. However, it contributes to more excitement in the cancer field and more young scientists choosing cancer research over cardiovascular research.

There are three reasons why the best and brightest minds in biomedical science might choose to devote their careers to one disease over another, according to Dr James Eberwine, codirector of the prestigious Penn Genome Frontiers Institute. The first is what he calls the "Pied Piper" effect: a faculty mentor whose enthusiasm is infectious and inspiring. The second reason, he says, is having an emotional history with a particular disease, prompting "the motivation to try to help."

And there's a third driving force, Eberwine continues, "which I don't like as much, but which is there, and that's the available funding. There are certain diseases that have captured the attention of the public and the [US] National Institutes of Health [NIH] beyond the attention of other things, and those tend to have money associated with them," he explains. "So the opportunity to do the research in a particular field might be a driving force as well."

Whether the amount of available research funding can explain the surge in new cancer therapies approved or awaiting approval is uncertain. What's clear, however, is that the NIH, the "largest source of funding for medical research in the world," allots significantly more funds to its National Cancer Institute (NCI) than it does the National Heart, Lung, and Blood Institute (NHLBI). From its 2010 budget of $30.9 billion, plus the NIH injection of $1.56 billion in funds from the American Recovery & Reinvestment Act (ARRA), just 7.8% of overall funding was earmarked for cardiovascular disease research; 20.3% was granted to cancer.

It's a disparity that rankles with the American Heart Association (AHA), which points out that heart disease remains the number-one killer of Americans, while cancer occupies the number-two position. And incoming president Dr Donna Arnett (University of Alabama at Birmingham) sees that discrepancy as a key reason that new research into cancer therapeutics may be pulling ahead of cardiovascular disease.

Passionate mentors and emotional motivators play a role, she says, "But I honestly think that when you get to the level of a PhD student or an MD/PhD student, that [the choice is] really driven by where you get money to train. And because the NCI budget is higher than the NHLBI's, there is much more opportunity for training."

The Numbers Game

Leaving aside the ARRA numbers, the actual NIH dollar amounts shake out as follows. In the 2010 fiscal year, the NHLBI was granted an operating budget of $3,093 billion, of which $1.320 billion went toward research project grants in the cardiovascular sciences and an additional $450 million toward specialized cardiac centers, other research, contracts, and training programs (the remainder was spent in similar ways for blood and lung disorders). By contrast, the NCI received $5,098 billion from the NIH pot, of which 42.5%, or $2,168 billion, was spent funding research grants, and the remainder toward specialized centers, research, contracts, intramural research, and other support.

As NHLBI acting director Dr Susan Shurin points out, it is the US Senate's Appropriations Committee that determines how the NIH budget is divvied up between institutes, based largely on prior year's budgets and emerging needs. And she balks at the idea that funding for the diseases should be decided by medical need—the fact that heart disease is the nation's number-one killer does not mean the NHBLI deserves the lion's share of NIH funding.

We don't consider ourselves in competition with cancer.
. . . Many of the things that cause people to get cancer
also cause people to get heart disease.

For one thing, she notes, stroke research is largely funded out of the National Institute of Neurological Disorders and Stroke, while projects within both cancer and cardiovascular disease might actually be funded out of the National Human Genome Research Institute or the institutes covering aging, diabetes, or environmental health.

"We don't consider ourselves in competition with cancer," says Shurin. "Many of the things that cause people to get cancer also cause people to get heart disease."

Besides, she says, some of the most important scientific advances come from the study of rare diseases. If government spending were determined solely based on the size of the population in need, funding might be better spent on public health over research or research targeting lower-income Americans and minority groups.

"I'm not saying we wouldn't like more money [for the NHLBI]," Shurin told *heartwire*. "I'm just saying that I worry when people talk about the idea that allocation ought to be on the number of people who are affected. It's the scientific opportunities that you want to pursue, and you're not always going to know where those are going to be."

More Cancer Researchers Ask for Money than Do Heart Researchers

But if researchers, perhaps even subconsciously, were drawn toward a bigger pot of research dollars, that might show up in the number of new grant applications reviewed by the respective institutes each year. And indeed, in 2010, 7338 research project grants were submitted and reviewed by the NCI—62% more than were submitted and reviewed by the NHLBI, at 4528. In total, 903 of those sent to the NHLBI were ultimately funded, yielding a success rate of almost 20%, as compared with 1253 funded by the NCI, a success rate of 17%.

Dr Clyde Yancy (Northwestern University, Chicago, IL), who spoke out about what he saw as inadequate NHLBI funding when he was AHA president, told *heartwire* he worries that young scientists may be dissuaded, in part, from pursuing a career in cardiovascular sciences precisely because the heart-disease arena has already seen some blockbuster therapies in recent decades, coupled with a corresponding improvement in disease survival.

"There is a sense that the CV [cardiovascular] space is overpopulated," he admits, but stresses that funding also plays a powerful role: "I think that expression of 'going where the money is' matters in this circumstance," he says.

"Depending on what kind of thought process, what kind of philosophy, what kind of political persuasion underpins the statements that are generated to the public with regard to requests for funding proposals (RFPs), this will generate the kinds of responses," he explains. "So part of the reason there may be so many more grants submitted to the cancer institute is because people see opportunities and gravitate toward oncology, but there also could be a certain sense that the NCI has the flexibility to introduce more RFPs."

Shurin points out that while the overall NIH budget has increased over time, the actual "buying power" of the NIH funding granted this year is at the same level as it was back in 2000 and 2001.

"The NHLBI is funding 8% fewer grants than we did last year, and the NCI is funding 15% fewer than it did last year," she said. "Believe me, I'm not telling you we don't need more money [for the NHLBI]: we really need more money. But the question is: what are the therapeutic opportunities that are not being pursued in heart disease? And I think there are fewer than there used to be, because some of this reflects that we have had some level of success."

But both Yancy and Shurin are adamant that the solution doesn't lie in sharing NIH funds more equitably between cancer and heart disease.

"Underfunding affects every area, and I would hate to be in a position in which we were cannibalizing one area of research in order to support another. I would not advocate reallocating funds that go toward cancer; I would strongly advocate funding research better," says Shurin. "And you can't throw money at a problem and expect to solve it, and you can see that in cancer. We've thrown a lot of money at cancer; we haven't solved a lot of the problems."

Yancy, likewise, insisted that the coffers for cardiovascular disease research can't be expanded "by shifting funds away from other very compelling diseases that have even larger unmet needs than we do." Instead, a greater commitment to biomedical research is needed, he says.

"Too many people get into this space and it becomes a tug of war, and it shouldn't be a tug of war; it should be a complementary discussion."

Nonprofit Groups Also Raise Money for Research

Of course, the NIH is only one source of funding for heart and cancer research: dedicated societies for both diseases also fundraise aggressively for their organizations and allocate a portion of that money for research via grant submission and peer-review processes.

Heart-disease research needs a breakthrough discovery . . . to reinvigorate the field.

Here again, the numbers are at odds, although the gap is much smaller. In the 2010 fiscal year, the AHA spent $114.8 million on research (19.4% of its total budget) while the American Cancer Society spent $148.6 million (16% of its budget). Of note, research funding by both groups was actually more similar in 2009: $142.7 million for the AHA and $149.8 million for the ACS. The American College of Cardiology spent half a million dollars on CVD research grants in 2010.

Arnett thinks heart-disease research needs a breakthrough discovery, in a new area, a stint on the marquee, to reinvigorate the field and points to some of the excitement bubbling in the areas of tissue engineering, embryonic or pluripotent stem cells, pharmacogenetics, nanotechnology, and bioengineering.

"There are so many cool things going on in cardiovascular disease right now," she says. "It's hard to believe that people think everything's been done."

Both the NIH numbers, determined by politicians, and the funds raised by nonprofit groups suggest that there are some even more fundamental, less tangible forces at play that push cancer ahead of cardiovascular disease.

Organizations to Contact

The editors have compiled the following list of organizations concerned with the issues debated in this book. The descriptions are derived from materials provided by the organizations. All have publications or information available for interested readers. The list was compiled on the date of publication of the present volume; the information provided here may change. Be aware that many organizations take several weeks or longer to respond to inquiries, so allow as much time as possible.

Alliance for Natural Health USA
1350 Connecticut Ave. NW, 5th Floor, Washington, DC   20036
(800) 230-2762 • fax: (202) 315-5837
website: www.anh-usa.org

The Alliance for Natural Health USA (ANH-USA) is part of an international organization dedicated to promoting sustainable health and freedom of choice in healthcare. The organization's mission is to protect the right of natural-health practitioners to practice and the right of consumers to choose the healthcare options they prefer. ANH-USA works to shift the medical paradigm from an exclusive focus on surgery, drugs, and other conventional techniques to an "integrative" approach incorporating functional foods, dietary supplements, and lifestyle changes. The organization's website provides a blog and a reader's corner where questions can be asked and answered. The ANH-USA also publishes a weekly electronic newsletter, the *Pulse of Natural Health*.

American Association for Cancer Research
615 Chestnut St., 17th Floor, Philadelphia, PA   19106
(215) 440-9300 • fax: (215) 440-9313
e-mail: aacr@aacr.org
website: www.aacr.org

The American Association for Cancer Research (AACR) is one of the oldest professional associations devoted to cancer research. AACR's mission is to prevent and cure cancer through research, education, communication, and collaboration. Through its programs and services, the AACR fosters research in cancer and related biomedical science; accelerates the dissemination of new research findings among scientists and others dedicated to the conquest of cancer; promotes science education and training; and advances the understanding of cancer etiology, prevention, diagnosis, and treatment throughout the world. The AACR is the scientific partner of *Stand Up To Cancer*, a collaboration of the entertainment industry. AACR publishes *CR* magazine.

American Cancer Society

250 Williams Street NW, Atlanta, GA 30303
(800) 227-2345 • fax: (404) 329-5787
website: www.cancer.org

The American Cancer Society (ACS) is a nationwide, community-based, voluntary health organization dedicated to eliminating cancer as a major health problem by preventing cancer, saving lives, and diminishing suffering from cancer, through research, education, advocacy, and service. The ACS publishes three peer-reviewed scientific periodicals, *CA: A Cancer Journal for Clinicians, Cancer*, and *Cancer Cytopathology*.

American Institute for Cancer Research

1759 R Street NW, Washington, DC 20009
(800) 843-8114 • fax: (202) 328-7226
e-mail: aicrweb@aicr.org
website: www.aicr.org

The American Institute for Cancer Research (AICR) is a nonprofit organization that works to create awareness of the relationship between diet and cancer risk, focuses funding on research into diet and cancer prevention, and consolidates and interprets global research to create a practical message on cancer prevention. To accomplish its mission the AICR funds research on the relationship of nutrition, physical activity and weight management to cancer risk, interprets the accumulated scientific literature in the field, and educates people about choices they can make to reduce their chances of developing cancer. The AICR offers many publications including, *The New American Plate, AICR Newsletter,* and *Science Now.*

CancerCare

275 Seventh Ave., 22nd Floor, New York, NY   10001
(800) 813-4673
e-mail: info@cancercare.org
website: www.cancercare.org

CancerCare is a nonprofit organization comprised of oncology social workers who provide free professional support services to individuals, families, caregivers, and the bereaved to help them better cope with and manage the emotional and practical challenges arising from cancer. CancerCare provides counseling and support groups, educational publications and workshops, and financial assistance. CancerCare's website provides booklets and fact sheets about cancer as well as personal stories of individuals with cancer and their loved ones.

Coalition of Cancer Cooperative Groups

1818 Market St., Suite 1100, Philadelphia, PA   19103
(877) 520-4457 • fax: (215) 789-3655
e-mail: Info@CancerTrialsHelp.org
website: www.cancertrialshelp.org

The Coalition of Cancer Cooperative Groups is a nonprofit organization with the mission of improving patient awareness of cancer clinical trials, facilitating access to cancer trails, and promoting participation in the trials. Through innovative programs and services, the Coalition examines and confronts key issues impeding cancer research. The Coalition website offers educational materials, patient stories, and a *Cancer Clinical Trials Blog.*

I Care I Cure Childhood Cancer Foundation

10433 S. Lake Vista Circle, Davie, FL   33328
(800) 807-8013

e-mail: info@icareicure.org
website: www.icareicure.org

The I Care I Cure Childhood Cancer Foundation is a non-profit organization supporting the development of, and raising public awareness about, cutting-edge, targeted therapies for childhood cancer. The goal of the Foundation is to make the treatment of childhood cancer gentler and more tolerable and to challenge the public's acceptance that treatment for childhood cancer requires painful and embarrassing side-effects and life-long health disabilities, isolation from friends and family, and short and long-term psychological devastation. The Foundation educates the public about scientific breakthroughs in genetic childhood cancer research and raises money to fund research grants and provide seed money to researchers for new studies. I Care I Cure has an electronic newsletter and a blog.

Lance Armstrong Foundation (Livestrong)

2201 E. Sixth Street, Austin, TX   78702
(877) 236-8820
website: www.livestrong.org

The Lance Armstrong Foundation, known as Livestrong, works to create a relevant, vibrant cancer movement. The organization raises awareness, increases outreach and facilitates collaboration in an effort to improve the cancer experience. The Survivor Empowerment Initiative, the Anti-Stigma Campaign, and Planet Cancer, are some of the campaigns and initiatives Livestrong uses to help cancer patients and cancer survivors. The Foundation speaks to the cancer community through the *Livestrong* quarterly magazine, as well as through Livestrong website and blog.

National Cancer Institute

NCI Office of Communications and Education
Public Inquiries Office, 6116 Executive Blvd., Suite 300
Bethesda, MD   20892

(800) 422-6237
website: www.cancer.gov

The National Cancer Institute (NCI) is one of the 27 Institutes and Centers that comprise the National Institutes of Health. The NCI coordinates the National Cancer Program, which conducts and supports research, training, health information dissemination, and other programs with respect to the cause, diagnosis, prevention, and treatment of cancer, rehabilitation from cancer, and the continuing care of cancer patients and the families of cancer patients. The NCI conducts research in its own laboratories and clinics and collaborates with voluntary organizations and other national and foreign institutions engaged in cancer research and training activities. The Institute publishes a biweekly newsletter, the *NCI Cancer Bulletin* to provide useful, timely information about cancer research to the cancer community.

National Foundation for Cancer Research
4600 East West Highway, Suite 525, Bethesda, MD   20814
(800) 321-2873 • fax: (301) 654-5824
e-mail: info@nfcr.org
website: www.nfcr.org

The National Foundation for Cancer Research (NFCR) is a nonprofit organization committed to supporting discovery-oriented scientific research for all types of cancer. The NFCR believes that in order to fully conquer cancer, innovative scientists must be encouraged to study cancer at its most fundamental level. Towards that end, the organization provides seed funding for innovative research that would not be funded otherwise, facilitates and fosters collaboration among scientists, serves as a catalyst to accelerate life-saving research, acts a bridge connecting scientist in their laboratories around the world in the pursuit of a cure for cancer, encourages scientists from different fields to join forces to accelerate the pace of cancer research, and demonstrates a long-term vision and commitment to cancer research. The NFCR provides several resources including a monthly electronic newsletter, the NFCR

On Your Health Series, the *To Your Health Cancer-Fighting Cookbook*, and other cancer-related materials.

Prevent Cancer Foundation

1600 Duke St., Suite 500, Alexandria, VA   22314
(703) 836-4412 • fax: (703) 836-4413
e-mail: pcf@preventcancer.org
website: www.preventcancer.org

The Prevent Cancer Foundation is a nonprofit organization dedicated to supporting cancer prevention research, education and outreach programs nationwide. The Foundation provides grants and fellowships to scientists researching cancer prevention and early detection and supports public education programs to help individuals understand the value of cancer screenings and healthy lifestyles. The Foundation also partners with local communities to implement life-saving cancer prevention and early detection programs. The website of the organization offers a blog and provides brochures and cancer prevention guides.

Bibliography

Books

Robert Aronowitz   *Unnatural History: Breast Cancer and American Society*, New York: Cambridge University Press, 2007.

Nancy Brinker and Joni Rodgers   *Promise Me: How a Sister's Love Launched the Global Movement to End Breast Cancer*, New York: Crown Archetype, 2010.

Helen S. L. Chan   *Understanding Cancer Therapies*, Jackson: University Press of Mississippi, 2007.

Mary Disis   *Immunotherapy of Cancer*, Totowa, NJ: Humana Press, 2006.

William L. Farrar   *Cancer Stem Cells*, New York: Cambridge University Press, 2009.

Brian Fies   *Mom's Cancer*, New York: Abrams ComicArts, 2006.

Maria Elizabeth Hewitt and Patricia Ganz   *From Cancer Patient to Cancer Survivor: Lost in Transition*, Washington, DC: National Academies Press, 2005.

Kelly Hunt, Stephan Vorgurger, and Stephen Swisher, eds.   *Gene Therapy for Cancer*, Totowa, NJ: Humana Press, 2007.

Shobha S. Krishnan

The HPV Vaccine Controversy: Sex, Cancer, God, and Politics: A Guide for Parents, Women Men, and Teenagers, Westport, CT: Praeger, 2008.

Lance Armstrong Foundation

Live Strong: Inspirational Stories From Cancer Survivors—From Diagnosis to Treatment and Beyond, New York: Broadway Books, 2005.

Sabrina McCormick

No Family History: The Environmental Links to Breast Cancer, Lanham, MD: Rowman & Littlefield Publishers, 2010.

Siddhartha Mukherjee

The Emperor of All Maladies: A Biography of Cancer, New York: Scribner, 2010.

Joseph Panno

Cancer: The Role of Genes, Lifestyle, and Environment, New York: Facts On File, 2005.

Julie K. Silver

After Cancer Treatment: Heal Faster, Better, Stronger, Baltimore: Johns Hopkins University Press, 2006.

Gayle Sulik

Pink Ribbon Blues: How Breast Cancer Culture Undermines Women's Health, New York: Oxford University Press, 2010.

World Cancer Research Fund/American Institute for Cancer Research — *Food, Nutrition, Physical Activity, and the Prevention of Cancer: A Global Perspective*, Washington, DC: World Cancer Research Fund/American Institute for Cancer Research, 2007.

Periodicals and Internet Sources

Jill Adams — "Cancer Drug Doxil Joins Growing List of Drugs in Short Supply," *Los Angeles Times*, November 14, 2011.

Sharon Begley — "A Medical Gamble," *Newsweek*, October 10, 2011.

Michael Behar — "Could This Kill Cancer?" *The Daily Beast*, November 21, 2010. www.the dailybeast.com.

Rebecca Boyle — "In First Clinical Trial, Unemployed Rattlesnakes Find Work as Cancer-Fighters," *Popular Science*, November 17, 2011.

Michael Brooks — "Master of the Cell," *New Statesman*, June 6, 2011.

Kiera Butler — "Sunscreen's Shady Business," *Mother Jones*, July/August 2009.

Trevor Butterworth — "Breast Cancer Fund's Scary Thanksgiving Study Is a Turkey," *Forbes*, November 16, 2011.

Nalini Chilkov   "Why 80 Percent of Cancer Patients Use Integrative Medicine," *Huffington Post*, March 23, 2011. www .huffingtonpost.com.

Jeannie Crofts   "Top Pathologist Looks at Future of Technology for Breast Cancer Research," *Medill Reports*, November 16, 2011.

A. Rosalie David and Michael R. Zimmerman   "Cancer: an Old Disease, a New Disease or Something in Between?" *Nature Reviews Cancer*, Vol. 10, October 2010.

Jacques Ferlay, Hai-Rim Shin, Freddie Bray, David Forman, Colin Mathers, and Donald Maxwell Parkin   "Estimates of Worldwide Burden of Cancer in 2008: GLOBOCAN 2008," *International Journal of Cancer*, December 15, 2010.

Chris Flemings   "U.S. Approves Cancer Drugs Faster than Europe," *Health Affairs Blog*, June 16, 2011. http://healthaffairs.org.

David H. Freedman   "The Triumph of New-Age Medicine," *Atlantic*, July 2011.

Jenifer Goodwin   "Cancer Doctors Still Not Great with Patients' Pain," *HealthDay News*, November 17, 2011.

Douglas Hanahan and Robert A. Weinberg   "Hallmarks of Cancer: The Next Generation," *Cell*, March 4, 2011.

Melissa Kite   "Research Sickness: Is There Anything Left That Doesn't Give You Cancer?" *Spectator*, August 6, 2011.

Kathiann M. Kowalski   "Radiation: What You Need to Know: Nuclear Radiation Can Affect Our Health—For Better or Worse," *Current Health Teens*, October 2011.

Elizabeth Landau   "Choosing Death Can Be Like a 'Birth,' Advocates Say," *CNN*, August 30, 2011.

Lauran Neergaard   "Rethinking Cancer Screening: Who Should Get Tested and Why?" *Associated Press*, November 9, 2011.

Shari Roan   "Promising Cancer Therapy Is Based on Epigenetics," *Los Angeles Times*, November 9, 2011.

Bonnie Rochman   "When Your Doctor Is a Rock Star: Oncologists Make Music for Cancer," *Time*, November 16, 2011.

Seth Rogan   "The Comedy of Cancer," *Newsweek*, October 3, 2011.

Nirvi Shah   "Debate Revives Old Arguments on HPV Vaccine," *Education Week*, September 28, 2011.

Rebecca Siegel, Elizabeth Ward, Otis Brawley, and Ahmedin Jemal   "Cancer Statistics 2011," *CA: A Cancer Journal for Clinicians*, July/August 2011.

Index

A

Ability to pay, 64
Access to treatment
    ethics issues, 63–64
    regional differences, 64
Acquired mutations, 12
Acupuncture, 47
Adult T-cell leukemia, 7
Age issues
    access to treatment, 64
    longer lives and more cancer,
    66–67
    mammograms, 28–31, 32,
    37–38
Aggressive vs. lifestyle/spirituality-
focused treatment, 41–47
Alcohol consumption, 19
Alliance for Natural Health
(ANH) USA, 41
American Academy of Pediatrics,
7
American Cancer Society, 7, 64,
65, 67, 78
American College of Cardiology,
78
American Heart Association, 74,
76, 78
American medical system
    breast cancer screening opin-
    ions, 33–36, 37–40
    cancer treatment, 41–42
    See also Funding, cancer re-
    search
American Recovery & Reinvest-
ment Act (ARRA) (2009), 74
American Society of Clinical On-
cology (ASCO), 10–13, 62

Ancient medicine, 16
Ancient societies, cancer studies,
    14–16
Animal products, consumption, 19
Antibodies, vaccines use, 8–9
Apoptosis (cell death), 12, 18, 21,
    51
Arnett, Donna, 74, 78
Artificial intelligence, 48–57
Autonomy, 63
Avastin (drug), 43

B

Bachmann, Michele, 7
Bacteria, 7
Beneficence principle, 63, 64
Blackmer, Jeff, 63, 64
Bladder cancer, 7
Brawley, Otis, 65
BRCA1 and BRCA2 genes, 12
Breast cancer
    diagnosis errors, 32, 39–40
    mammograms can save lives,
    28–31
    mammograms do not save
    lives, 32–40
    patient studies, 25–26
    prevention/vitamin D, 18, 20,
    21, 22, 23, 24, 25–26
    research and therapies, 65–66
    research funding, 35, 36, 69,
    70
    surgery, 43–44
    survival rates, 22, 69, 71
    treatments, 32, 36, 37
Breast cancer survivors, 35, 36
Breast self-examinations, 29, 39

C

Calcitriol, 21

Calcium, 21–22, 26

Canada, cancer care, 59–64, 65, 66, 68

Canada Health Act (1984), 64

Canadian Cancer Society, 65

Canadian Partnership Against Cancer, 61

"Cancer: an old disease, a new disease or something in between?" (study; David and Zimmerman), 14–16

Cancer Commons (application), 48, 49–50, 53–57

Cancer drugs, 43, 49, 51–53, 59–60, 65

Cancer survivors, 35, 36
    care, 62–63
    quality of life, 60–61
    rates by cancer type, 71

Cannell, John, 18

Causes of cancer
    genes, 10–13, 51
    modern environment, 14–17, 18, 19, 44
    risk factors, 18, 19

Cell death, 12, 18, 21, 51

Cell division, 11, 51

Cell turnover, 11

Centers for Disease Control and Prevention (CDC), 23, 70

Cervical cancer
    human papilloma virus (HPV), 7
    prevention program funding, 70

Chemotherapy, 8
    as aggressive treatment, 41, 43
    breast cancer, 32, 36, 37
    side effects, 43, 46
    vs. targeted treatment, 51

Chromosomes, 10, 11

Chronic myelogenous leukemia, 52, 59

Clinical drug trials, 49, 51–52, 54

Clinical studies
    omega 3s and cancer, 24–25
    patient responses, and information sharing, 50, 53–57
    vitamin D and cancer, 21–22, 23, 24–27

Clinton, Steven K., 26

Coley's fluid, 47

Colon cancer
    patient studies, 25
    prevention/vitamin D, 18, 20, 21, 24, 25
    research and therapies, 65–66
    research funding, 70
    screening, 62
    survival rates, 22

Colson, Yolanda L., 69–72

Costs of cancer and care, 65–66, 68

Curing cancer
    artificial intelligence applications, 48–57
    multiple disease aspect, 50, 67
    pessimism, 14, 59
    process, and associated improvements, 57, 58–68
    timeframes, 58

D

Dairy consumption, 19

David, A. Rosalie, 14–16

Deaths from cancer
    income correlations, 64
    lung cancer, 69–70, 72
    projections, 18, 64, 67
    realities, 48, 64

regional/sunlight exposure differences, 19–20

Deaths from heart disease, 73, 74, 75

Deming, W. Edwards, 54–55

Deoxyribonucleic acid (DNA), 10

Department of Defense (DoD), 70

Diet
cancer risk factor, 18, 19, 45
as treatment, 41, 42, 45–46
See also Vitamin D

Disease populations, heterogeneous, 50–51

DNA repair genes, 10, 12

Doctor-patient relationships, 43, 60–61

Doll, Richard, 60–61

Drug trials, 49, 51–52, 54

E

Earle, Craig, 65–66, 68

Eberwine, James, 73–74

Ecological studies, 20

"The Economic Burden of Illness in Canada, 1998" (report), 65

Egypt, ancient peoples, 14–16

The Emperor of All Maladies, a Biography of Cancer (Mukherjee), 43, 45

Environment, as cause of cancer, 14–17, 18, 19, 44

Enzyme blocking, 52

Epstein-Barr virus, 7

Ethical dilemmas, 63–64

European cancer therapies, 47

Exercise, 45

F

False positives
breast cancer screenings, 29, 30, 32, 37, 39–40
cancer screenings, 44

Familial cancer, 12, 33, 39

FDA (US Food and Drug Administration), 8, 9

5-year survivals, 60, 71

Funding, cancer research, 70, 73–79
breast cancer, 35, 36, 69, 70
colorectal cancer, 70
vs. heart research, 73–79
lung cancer, 69–72
ovarian cancer, 70
prostate cancer, 69, 70
requests, 76–77

G

Gastrointestinal stromal tumors, 52

Genes, 10–11
cause of cancer, 10–13, 51
not cause of cancer, 14–17

Genetic cancer, 12, 33, 39

Genetic mutations, 11–12, 13

Genomics, 48, 49–57, 59, 60, 67

Germline mutations, 11–12

Gleevec (drug), 43, 52, 54, 59

Godkin, David, 58–68

Goldstein, Michael, 62

Grove, Andy, 55

H

Halsted, Richard, 43

Haseltine, William, 9

Health care system navigation, 62

Heart disease
    research, compared to cancer
      research, 73–79
    women, 35
Heat therapy, 47
Helicobacter pylori infections, 7
Hepatitis B and C viruses, 7
HER2/neu (oncogene), 12
Herceptin (drug), 43
Heterogeneous disease popula-
    tions, 50–51
Hodgkin's lymphoma, 7, 20
Homeopathic remedies, 41, 46–47
Human papilloma virus (HPV)
    inoculation, 7
Human resources, cancer care,
    61–63, 68
Hyperthermia therapy, 47

I

Immune systems
    healthy diets, 45
    vaccine effects, 8, 9
Immunotherapy, 8–9
Institute of Medicine (IOM), 23,
    24, 26
Insulin-like growth factor (IGF),
    19

J

Justice in medicine, 63–64

K

Kaposi's sarcoma, 7
Khullar, Onkar, 69–72
"Knowledge turns," 55
Kopans, Daniel B., 28–31

L

Leukemia
    adult, 7
    drug development/therapy, 52,
      59
    prevention, 20
Levy, David, 66
Life spans
    ancient peoples, 14, 15
    modern populations, 66, 67
Lifestyle, and cancer treatment,
    41–47
Light therapy, 47
Liver cancer, 7
Love, Susan, 34
Lung cancer
    drug therapies, 65
    nonsmokers, 71
    research is underfunded,
      69–72
    survival rates, 22, 69, 71
    women, 35
Lymphoma, 7, 20, 22, 42–43

M

Machine learning (ML), 48–57
Mammograms
    can save lives, 28–31
    costs, 31, 38
    do not save lives, 32–40
    personal stories, 33–34, 36
    screening frequency recom-
      mendations, 28–29, 30, 32,
      38
Manageability of cancer, 58–68
Management theory, 54–55
Manson, JoAnn E., 24, 25
Maroun, Jean, 59
Masson, Veneta, 32–40
MD Anderson Cancer Center, 46

Meat consumption, 19
Medicinal foods, 46
Melanoma
    drug development, 52, 54
    risk factors, 19–20
    survival rates, 22
Memorial Sloan Kettering Cancer
    Center, 46
Metastasis, 18
Microbes, 7–8
Mishra, Ruchika, 64
Mitchell, Mamie, 63
Modern environment, as cause of
    cancer, 14–17, 18, 19, 44
Molecular disease models and
    testing, 53–54, 55, 56, 65–66
Morris, Martha Clare, 26–27
Mukherjee, Siddhartha, 43
Multiple myeloma, 20
Mummies, study, 14, 15–16
Mutations
    drug function focus, 51, 60,
    65–66
    genetic, 11–12, 13
    germline, 11–12
    lung cancer, 71
    processes, 50–51

N

National Cancer Institute (NCI),
28, 31, 46, 70, 74, 75, 76, 77
National Heart, Lung, and Blood
    Institute (NHLBI), 74–76, 77
National Human Genome Re-
    search Institute, 75
National Institute of Neurological
    Disorders and Stroke, 75
National Institutes of Health
    (NIH), 24, 46, 70, 74–75, 77, 78,
    79
Nicholas, Joanne, 23–27

Non-Hodgkin's lymphoma, 20, 22
Non-maleficence principle, 63
Nonprofit research funding, 73,
    78–79
Nonsmokers with lung cancer, 71
Nordic Cochrane Centre, 35–36,
    37
Novartis, 52
Nurses, human resources, 61,
    62–63
Nutritional guidelines, 45–46

O

Obesity as risk factor, 18, 19
Observational studies, 20
Omega-3 fatty acids, 24–25
Oncogenes, 10, 12, 51
Oncologists, human resource to-
    tals, 61, 62
Ovarian cancer, research funding,
    70

P

p53 genes, 12
Pancreatic cancer, prevention, 24
Parliament, Matthew, 61–62
Pathogens, as vaccine components,
    8
Patient autonomy, 63
Patient information sharing, and
    curing cancer, 48, 49–50, 53–57
Penile cancer, 7
Perry, Rick, 7
Personalized medicine, 50–53,
    56–57
PET scans, 42
Pharmaceutical industry
    innovation advice, 55
    nature of trials, 49, 51–52

Phosphate groups, 51
Phototherapy, 47
Population aging, 66, 67
Prevention methods
    cervical cancer funding, 70
    exercise, 45
    healthy diet, 45–46
    mammograms can save lives,
      28–31
    mammograms do not save
      lives, 32–40
    screening, general, 44
    smoking cessation, 70–71
    vitamin D reduces risk, 18–22
    vitamin D role is unclear,
      23–27
Prostate cancer
    patient studies, 25
    prevention/vitamin D, 22, 23,
      24, 25
    research funding, 69, 70
    survival rates, 22, 69, 71
    vaccines, 8–9
Provenge (prostate cancer
    vaccine), 8–9

Q

Quality of life issues, 60–61, 68

R

Radiation therapy
    breast cancer, 36, 37
    Canadian treatment levels,
      61–62
    side effects, 46
ras (oncogene), 12
Ray, Deborah A., 41–47
Rectal cancer
    patient studies, 25
    prevention/vitamin D, 18, 20,
      21, 25

    research funding, 70
    screening, 62
    survival rates, 22
Regional differences, access to
    care, 64
Republican primary campaign,
    2011-2012, 7
Requests for funding proposals
    (RFPs), 76–77
Research. *See* Clinical drug trials;
    Funding, cancer research; Mo-
    lecular disease models and test-
    ing
Risk factors, 18, 19
    See also Causes of cancer

S

Sarcoma, 52
Self-examinations, 29, 39
Sex chromosomes, 11
Shrager, Jeff, 48–57
Shurin, Susan, 75–76, 77
Skin cancer, risk factors, 19–20
Smoking
    cancer deaths and, 64, 70–71
    cancer risk factor, 18, 19
Smoking cessation programs,
    70–71
Sonodynamic therapy, 47
Spirituality, and cancer treatment,
    41–47
Sporadic cancer, 12
Stevenson, Heidi, 14–17
Stomach cancer, 7
Strokes, 23, 25, 71, 75
Studies. *See* Clinical drug trials;
    Clinical studies
Sunburns, 19
Sunlight exposure, 17, 19–20

Supplements, vitamin D, 20, 22, 26
Surgery
    as aggressive treatment, 41, 43–44
    breast cancer, 43–44
Survival rates
    breast cancer, 22, 69, 71
    colon cancer, 22
    lung cancer, 22, 69, 71
    melanoma, 22
    prostate cancer, 22, 69, 71
    vitamin D intake, 22
"Survivorship," 60–61

T

Tangney, Christine C., 26
Targeted cancer therapies, 51
Taxol (drug), 43
Tenenbaum, Jay M., 48–57
Therapeutic cancer vaccines, 8
Throat cancer, 7
Tobacco use, and cancer deaths, 64, 70–71
Tremblay, Michel, 60
Tumor suppressor genes, 10, 12
Tumors
    growth, and diet, 19
    as limited view of cancer, 60–61
    tissue longevity, 14, 15, 16
    uniqueness, research, and treatment, 48, 49–57, 65–66, 67
    vitamin D effects, 21

U

Ultraviolet-B (UVB) light, 19, 20

US Department of Defense (DoD), 70
US Food and Drug Administration (FDA), 8, 9
US Preventive Services Task Force, 28–31, 37–38

V

Vaccination risk debate, 7
Vaccines, anti-cancer, 7–9
Vaginal cancer, 7
Viruses, 7
VITAL Trial, 23, 24–25
Vitamin C, 46
Vitamin D
    deficiencies, 17, 18, 23
    reduces risk of cancer, 18–22
    role in cancer prevention is unclear, 23–27
Vitamin D Council, 18–22
von Volkmann, Richard, 43

W

Wei, Alice, 59
Weiss, Glen, 59
Welch, Gilbert, 44
Whittom, Renaud, 61
Wiernikowski, Jennifer, 62–63
Wood, Shelley, 73–79
Wosnick, Michael, 59–60

Y

Yancy, Clyde, 76, 77

Z

Zimmerman, Michael R., 14–16